MW01204641

THERE IS LIFE AFTER LETTUCE

Delicious recipes for heart patients, diabetics, dieters, and everyone else

By
Pepper Durcholz
Alberta Gentry
Carolyn Williamson, M.S.

EAKIN PRESS ★ Austin, Texas

FIRST EDITION

Published in the United States of America
By Eakin Press
An Imprint of Sunbelt Media, Inc.
P.O. Drawer 90159 ★ Austin, TX 78709-0159

ISBN 0-89015-891-6

Library of Congress Cataloging-in-Publication Data

Williamson, Carolyn.
There is life after lettuce : delicious recipes for heart patients, diabetics, dieters, and everyone else / by Pepper Durcholz, Alberta Gentry, [written by] Carolyn Williamson. — 1st ed.
p. cm.
Includes index.
ISBN 0-89015-891-6 : $15.95
1. Reducing diet — Recipes. 2. Low-fat diet — Recipes. 3. Salt-free diet — Recipes. 4. Coronary heart disease — Diet therapy — Recipes. 5. Diabetes — Diet therapy — Recipes. I. Durcholz, Pepper. II. Gentry, Alberta. III. Title.
RM222.2.W4555 1993
641.5′63 — dc20 93-9548
CIP

To those with dietary restrictions,
whether by choice or by doctor's orders,
we dedicate this book in hopes it adds
weightless delights to their lives.

Contents

Acknowledgments

We wish to thank our families and friends, D.F.W. Writer's Workshop, Wordwranglers, N.T.R.W.A. and Dallas Area Romance Authors, who read our work and tasted the food made with our recipes.

Introduction

Healthy eating can be fun and delicious with these tasty, kitchen-tested recipes, certified low in fat, sugar, salt, and calories. Better yet, you can have a healthier, thinner life without marrying a lettuce farmer.

This book is different from other books because:

1. Most dishes take only minutes to prepare.
2. You can serve the same tasty food to your family.
3. Variety makes healthy eating easy to live with day after day.
4. Food plans are simple to use and easy to remember.
5. Food plans are based on good nutritional guidelines.
6. You can enjoy eating again and use the same basic pattern to maintain desirable weight for the rest of your life.

It is possible to adjust your way of eating, lose weight, and keep it off — with less trouble than you think. When you balance the calories you eat with daily activities, your weight will remain stable. These recipes will give you good-tasting food to help you become slimmer and healthier. All of them have been taste-tested by diabetics, heart patients, children, husbands, and friends.

How to Use This Book

For delicious recipes low in cholesterol, salt, fat, and calories, turn to Chapter 1. Chapter 2 has suggestions for heart patients, and ones for diabetics are in Chapter 3. Browse through Chapter 4 if you're interested in how heredity and life-style affect your weight. Simple, easy-to-follow food plans in Chapter 5 and menus with alternatives to suit your preferences are followed by helpful tips, which include ways to cut calories you'll never miss plus valuable hints for dining out.

For explanations of those complicated names for fats, see Appendix A. Food exchanges for diabetics, which are similar to those of Weight Watchers, are in Appendix B.

Carolyn Williamson, who has a master's degree in home economics and operated her own catering firm, wrote the text and developed recipes in collaboration with diabetic co-authors, Pepper Durcholz and Alberta Gentry.

1.

Palate-pleasing Recipes

This chapter has easy-to-prepare recipes to please your whole family. Many helpful tips are sprinkled throughout the recipe pages.

Fat, sugar, salt, and cholesterol have been cut down to a minimum. At the end of each recipe are listed calorie, fat, cholesterol, carbohydrate, and sodium amounts, along with food exchanges for diabetics, which are similar to those used by Weight Watchers.

Fruit and sometimes a very small amount of sugar have been spread over a large recipe to develop good breads, muffins, coffee cakes, and desserts. (It is possible to make sugarless cakes, but as a rule they are unsatisfactory.) According to dietitians, this small amount of sugar (1 tsp. per serving) can generally be tolerated by diabetics if they eat only one serving of such food at a meal.

Reducing the amount of sugar often makes the tops of baked items less brown, so bake until the crust springs back slightly when touched. Baked goods with only a small amount of sugar sometimes spoil more rapidly, so you may wish to refrigerate the uneaten part.

Many sweeteners on the market today tend to break down when cooked at boiling point or add an "off" taste when used in large amounts. This effect is less noticeable with the microwave. Therefore, foods may not turn out as well if you use a different sweetener or cooking method than suggested in the recipe.

Warning: Equal, made with aspartame, which contains two amino acids that occur naturally in foods, has been proven safe for the general public. However, those who are born with the hereditary condition called phenylketonuria should avoid Equal. Infants with this condition can't digest the amino acid phenylalanine, found in some protein foods, and can become mentally retarded if they eat foods containing that amino acid.

Cooking tips:

1. Use nonstick-surface pans and woks as much as possible.
2. Cook with the smallest possible amount of fat, and drain cooked meat in a colander or on a paper towel.
3. For stews and soups, refrigerate the food in a tall container. The fat will rise and harden so you can remove it and reheat the food.
4. If using fruit canned in syrup, drain the syrup off and rinse fruit. (The syrup contains sugar and hidden calories.)
5. Add Equal after removing food from heat, whenever possible.

Abbreviations used are: Tbs. = tablespoon, tsp. = teaspoon, lb. = pound, oz. = ounce, g = gram, mg = milligram.

Note: In Nutrients per serving, — indicates trace amounts.

Appetizers

MELON NIBBLES

1 large cantaloupe
1 large honeydew melon
1 3 oz. pkg. thinly sliced ham or turkey

Cut melons in half and remove seeds. Use a melon baller to scoop out pulp. Cut ham or turkey into 1-inch-wide strips. Wrap 1 strip of meat around each melon ball; fasten with a toothpick. Makes 60 servings (1 melon ball per serving).

Nutrients per ball:	
Calories	14
Fat	0
Cholesterol	0
Carbohydrate	3g
Sodium	20mg

Exchanges:	*6 balls*	*10 balls*
Meat	1/2	1
Fruit	1	1 1/3

BROILED STUFFED TOMATOES

1/4 cup green onion, minced
3 Tbs. green pepper, minced
1 cup fresh mushrooms, chopped
3 Tbs. celery, minced
4 medium tomatoes
1/4 tsp. basil
1 1/2 Tbs. artificial bacon bits
1 Tbs. Fleischmann's corn oil margarine

Cut tomatoes in half, scoop out the insides, and chop them up. Save insides and juice. Sauté the green onion, green pepper, and mushrooms together in margarine. Mix in celery, tomato pieces, and basil. Stuff tomato shells and sprinkle with artificial bacon bits. Broil 2–4 minutes until heated through. Makes 8 halves.

Nutrients per half:		Exchanges:	
Calories	28	Vegetable	1/2
Fat	1g		
Cholesterol	0		
Carbohydrate	3g		
Sodium	6mg		

Dip tomato in boiling water for easier peeling.

Raw fruits and vegetables have more useful fiber than cooked ones.

CRAB AND CHEDDAR ON RYE

6 oz. can lump crabmeat (Sealegs, imitation crabmeat okay)
1/2 cup sharp cheddar cheese, grated
1/3 cup Miracle Whip Light
2 shakes garlic powder (1/8 tsp. for triple recipe)
2 shakes Lea and Perrin Worcestershire Sauce (1/2 tsp. for triple recipe)
3 Tbs. thinly sliced green onion (about one onion including stem)
3/4 loaf party snack rye bread

Mix first six ingredients and spread on bread. Broil until it bubbles and has spots of delicate brown (about 1–2 minutes). Makes 20 appetizers.

Nutrients per serving:		Exchanges:	
Calories	32	Meat	1/2
Fat	2g	Vegetable	1
Cholesterol	12mg		
Carbohydrate	3g		
Sodium	132mg		

POPOVERS WITH TUNA, CHICKEN, OR CRAB FILLING

1 cup flour
1/4 tsp. salt
1 cup milk
1 egg and 2 egg whites

Preheat oven to 425. Beat ingredients together with egg beater or wire whisk, just until smooth. Grease 10 deep muffin cups and fill half full. Bake

35–45 minutes until puffed and golden brown. Let cool and slice in half. Fill with tuna or chicken filling; replace top and refrigerate until serving time. (*Note:* Do not skimp on batter and make more; popovers will not rise enough.)

Tuna filling:

3 cans water-packed tuna chunks
1 cup Miracle Whip Light
1 cup chopped celery
1/2 c. pickle relish (chopped sour pickles recommended for diabetics; if desired, sweeten with Equal)

Mix well. Makes enough for 3 popover recipes.

Always buy water-packed tuna.

Chicken filling:

1 cup chicken thighs (4), boiled in water until done, then cut up into small pieces
1/8 tsp. garlic powder
1/3 cup pickle relish or chopped pickles (relish high in sugar)
3 Tbs. Miracle Whip Light
1/3 cup chopped celery

Mix well. Add pickle juice if too dry. Makes enough for 10 popovers.

Crab filling:

1/3 cup Miracle Whip Light
2 Tbs. skim milk
1/3 cup minced celery
1/3 cup chopped green pepper
2 Tbs. minced green onion stems
1/2 lb. crab or imitation crabmeat, chopped

Mix Miracle Whip Light with 1 Tbs. skim milk until well blended. Repeat with the second Tbs. skim milk. Mix celery, green pepper, green onion stems, and crab. Stir in dressing. Just before serving, cut tops of popovers partly off, stuff with crab mixture, and push top back down. Makes enough for 20 popovers.

Nutrients per popover:

	Tuna	*Chicken*	*Crab*
Calories	108	114	78
Fat	2.5g	2.5g	2g
Cholesterol	43mg	49mg	27mg
Carbohydrate	13.3g	14.2g	11.4g
Sodium	238mg	207mg	111mg

Exchanges:			
Meat	1	1	1
Bread	1	1	1

STUFFED MUSHROOMS

1/2 pkg. frozen spinach
1/2 lb. large fresh mushrooms
1 Tbs. margarine
2 Tbs. cornstarch
3/4 cup evaporated skim milk
1/2 cup regular skim milk
1/4 tsp. salt substitute
1/2 cup ricotta cheese
1 Tbs. grated Parmesan cheese
Parsley flakes

Put unopened package of spinach in microwave and cook on high for 3 minutes. Let cool, then open one end and squeeze out liquid. Or cook on stove until no longer frozen and drain. Use 1/2 pkg. for this recipe.

Wash enough mushrooms to cover bottom of Corningware baking dish. Dry with paper towel. Remove stems and mince them. Melt margarine in small skillet and heat bottoms of mushroom caps for a short time. Put in baking dish. Add chopped stems to skillet and sauté for a few minutes. Mix cornstarch with a little of the milk until lumps are dissolved. Add remaining milk and pour the mixture into skillet. Cook, stirring constantly, until thickened. Add salt substitute. Remove from heat.

Mix spinach with ricotta cheese and stuff mushroom caps. Sprinkle with Parmesan cheese. Pour on sauce. Sprinkle with parsley flakes and bake until heated through, or microwave on high for 5 minutes. Serves 6 (about 2 caps and some sauce per serving).

Nutrients per serving:	
Calories	96
Fat	4g
Cholesterol	9mg
Carbohydrate	7g
Sodium	193mg

Exchanges:	
Milk	1/2
Vegetable	1
Fat	1

1 cup fresh mushrooms adds flavor to a dish for only 10 calories.

GREEK MEATBALLS

2 cans tomatoes (1 lb. 12 oz. each)
2 lbs. lean ground beef
4 medium onions, minced
2 cups Italian-style seasoned bread crumbs
1½ to 2 cups water
2 tsp. dried mint leaves
1 tsp. cinnamon
1 tsp. salt substitute
1/4 tsp. pepper
1/2 tsp. cinnamon (sprinkle on top)

Purée tomatoes in blender 1 minute. Mix other ingredients except 1/2 tsp. cinnamon. Add water gradually. If mixture becomes soupy, don't use all the water. Make 160 meatballs about the size of a walnut. Place in a shallow pan. Cover with tomato mixture. Sprinkle with 1/2 tsp. cinnamon. Bake uncovered at 400 degrees for an hour. Turn once while baking. (1 serving = two balls.)

Nutrients per serving:	
Calories	47
Fat	2g
Cholesterol	10mg
Carbohydrate	3g
Sodium	88mg

Exchanges:	
Meat	1/2
Bread	1/4

MARINATED BEEF SHISHKABOBS

1/3 lb. sirloin or rib steak (1 large sirloin steak makes 50), cut in 20 one-inch cubes for 20 appetizers
1/2 of a green pepper cut into 20 squares
1/2 bottle cocktail onions (3½ oz. size)
1 bottle (2½ oz.) button mushrooms or 20 small fresh ones

Marinade: (use 6 times this for 200 appetizers)

1/2 cup burgundy wine
1 tsp. Worcestershire sauce
1 tsp. garlic powder
1/2 cup vegetable oil
2 Tbs. catsup
1 tsp. sugar
1/2 tsp. monosodium glutamate (Accent)
1 Tbs. vingegar
1/2 tsp. marjoram leaves
1/2 tsp. rosemary leaves

Mix marinade and put in baking pan with deep sides. Cut meat into cubes. Place one cube on toothpick. Add a square of green pepper (cut 3/4-inch size), a cocktail onion and a mushroom cap. Let sit in marinade one day, basting with marinade occasionally. Broil 1 minute. Serve hot. Makes 20. (1 serving = 3.)

Nutrients per serving:		Exchanges:	
Calories	129	Meat	1
Fat	10g	Vegetable	1/2
Cholesterol	26mg	Fat	1
Carbohydrate	2g		
Sodium	24mg		

GREEN ONION DIP

1 lb. lowfat cottage cheese (1% fat)
1/4 tsp. Worcestershire sauce (Lea & Perrin's)
1/4 cup thinly sliced green onions (including stems)
3–4 Tbs. skim milk, optional — use as needed to thin dip
1/4 tsp. garlic powder
1/2 tsp. salt substitute

Mix in blender until smooth. Chill for 2 hours. Makes 64 servings of 1 Tbs. each.

Nutrients per 4 servings:		Exchanges:	
Calories	7.6	Meat	1/2
Fat	.24g		
Cholesterol	1mg		
Carbohydrate	2g		
Sodium	36mg		

CALORIE CHEATER'S CHIPS

Cut soft cornmeal tortillas into 8 triangles. Bake at 375 degrees for 10 minutes or until crisp. Serve with picante sauce or above dip. Low-salt Wheat Thins can also be substituted for potato chips. (Four triangles = 1 serving.)

Nutrients per serving:		Exchanges:	
Calories	32	Bread	1/2
Fat	.5g		
Cholesterol	0		
Carbohydrate	6.5g		
Sodium	1mg		

FRUIT DIP

1 cup cottage cheese
1 medium banana
2 pkg. Equal
1/2 tsp nutmeg
1 tsp. cinnamon

Mix ingredients in blender until smooth. Serve as dip for pieces of raw fruit. (1 serving = 2 Tbs.)

Nutrients per serving:		Exchanges:	
Calories	26	Milk	1/3
Fat	.5g		
Cholesterol	1.6mg		
Carbohydrate	3.2g		
Sodium	76mg		

GUACAMOLE DIP

1 large avocado
1/2 cup green onions, finely sliced
1/4 tsp. garlic powder
2 cups lowfat yogurt (Dannon)

Peel avocado and cut in pieces. Put all ingredients in blender and blend well. Chill until serving time.

Nutrients per 1 tsp.:		Exchanges:	
Calories	17	Bread	1/8
Fat	1.5g	Fat	1/4
Cholesterol	.5mg		
Carbohydrate	1.6g		
Sodium	12mg		

MILD CHILI SAUCE

1/3 cup green onions, thinly sliced
1 garlic clove, minced
1/4 tsp. hot chili paste
1/2 cup white vinegar
1/4 tsp. sesame oil

Combine all ingredients in a bowl and stir well. Store in refrigerator in airtight container. Yields about 2/3 cup. (1 tsp. per serving.)

Nutrients per serving:		Exchanges:
Calorie	1	Free up to 20 tsp.
Fat	0	
Cholesterol	0	
Carbohydrate	.3g	
Sodium	2mg	

Substitute lowfat yogurt for sour cream in dip recipes.

Beverages

LEMON LIME FLOAT

1 can lemon-lime diet soft drink such as Sprite

1/4 cup frozen La Creme or Cool Whip

Put frozen whipped topping in tall glass. Add soda and stir. For variety, add *one* drop of peppermint extract.

Nutrients per serving:	
Calories	50
Fat	4g
Cholesterol	0
Carbohydrate	4g
Sodium	31mg

Exchanges:	
Milk	1/2

VICKI'S PINEAPPLE FROSTY

12 oz. frozen natural pineapple juice

4 sliced frozen bananas

4 Tbs. coconut

1 cup plain yogurt, lowfat

Put half of banana in blender and blend with other ingredients. Add rest of banana and blend. Serves 7. (From Vicki Harrold.)

Nutrients per serving:	
Calories	123
Fat	2g
Cholesterol	2g
Carbohydrate	29g
Sodium	31mg

Exchanges:	
Fruit	$1\frac{1}{2}$
Milk	1/4

Note: For maximum flavor in your frosties, be sure all ingredients are chilled and fruits are very ripe. This can be frozen and served as a dessert.

VICKI'S CRANBERRY YOGURT MILKSHAKE

1 cup cranapple juice
1/2 cup nonfat yogurt
10 frozen strawberries
4 pkg. Equal

Mix in blender. Serves 2. (From Vicki Harrold.)

Nutrients per Serving:		Exchanges:	
Calories	185	Fruit	2 1/2
Fat	0	Milk	1/2
Cholesterol	0		
Carbohydrate	44g		
Sodium	47mg		

LITE HOT CHOCOLATE FOR ONE

1 heaping tsp. cocoa
1/2 cup skim milk
1/2 cup water
Drop vanilla
3 packets Equal

Put cocoa in large mug and shake in 1 dash salt. Add 1–2 Tbs. milk and mix well. Add rest of milk. Mix well. Add water and stir. Do not fill mug beyond 1 inch from top of cup. Heat in microwave for 1 minute. If not hot enough, heat for another minute. Add a drop of vanilla and 2 or 3 packets Equal and stir. If not sweet enough, add more Equal. Makes one 3/4 cup serving.

Nutrients per serving:		Exchanges:	
Calories	52	Milk	3/4
Fat	0		
Cholesterol	1.5mg		
Carbohydrate	8.1g		
Sodium	47mg		

HOT LEMON TEA

1 level tsp. low calorie tea with lemon/sweetener
1 rounded tsp. SugarTwin
1/2 tsp. Realemon juice
Few shakes nutmeg
1 mug of boiling water

Put first 4 ingredients in mug. Add boiling water and stir.

Nutrients per serving:	Exchanges:
Approx. 5 calories	Free

HOT LEMON PEPPER

1 can Diet Dr. Pepper

Lemon juice to taste

Heat Diet Dr. Pepper in a saucepan until just hot; don't boil. Pour into cups. Add lemon juice to taste. Serves 2.

Nutrients per serving:		Exchanges:
Calories	Less than 1 per cup	Free
Fat	0	
Cholesterol	0	
Carbohydrate	0	
Sodium	0	

Freeze a drop or two of lemon juice in each ice cube for your tea. Good in water too.

ORANGE SUMMER COOLER
"Frosty Fruity"

1 cup unsweetened orange juice
3/4 cup crushed ice or 6 ice cubes
1/2 cup unsweetened fresh or frozen strawberries
1 medium banana
1 pkg. Equal

Whip all ingredients in blender for 30 to 60 seconds. Pour into tall glasses. Serves 4; makes about 2¾ cups. (Serving size 2/3 cup.)

Nutrients per serving:		Exchanges:	
Calories	61	Fruit	1
Fat	1g		
Cholesterol	0		
Carbohydrate	15g		
Sodium	1mg		

BANANA MILKSHAKE

1 medium banana, ripe
1/4 cup skim milk
1/2 tsp. vanilla
1 pkg. Equal

Slice banana and put into a blender. Add other ingredients. Blend and pour into glass. Serves 1.

Nutrients per serving:		Exchanges:	
Calories	122	Fruit	2
Fat	.5g	Milk	1/4
Cholesterol	0		
Carbohydrate	30g		
Sodium	0		

BANANA LIME COOLER

1 banana, cut up
1 lime
1 cup skim milk
6 pkg. Sweet 'N Low

Blend well in a blender. Makes 2 servings.

Nutrients per serving:		Exchanges:	
Calories	115	Fruit	1 1/2
Fat	.5g	Milk	1/2
Cholesterol	2mg		
Carbohydrate	25.3g		
Sodium	63.75 mg		

FROSTY PEACH COOLER

1 fresh, ripe peach, peeled and sliced
1/4 tsp. lime juice
1/4 cup water
3 Tbs. frozen orange juice concentrate (unsweetened)
1/2 cup crushed ice
1 12-oz. can lemon-lime flavored carbonated drink (Sugar-free)

Whip sliced peach, lime juice, water, orange juice concentrate, and crushed ice in blender until smooth and frosty. Pour over ice cubes in tall glass until half full. Fizz with carbonated beverage and stir gently. Serves 5; about 3½ c. (Serving size is 3/4 cup.)

Note: Any other fruit may be substituted for peach.

Nutrients per serving:		Exchanges:	
Calories	37	Fruit	1/2
Fat	trace		
Cholesterol	0		
Carbohydrate	9g		
Sodium	1mg		

TROPICAL DRINK

8 oz. crushed pineapple, canned in own juice
1 cup Yoplait vanilla nonfat yogurt
1 banana
1/2 cup skim milk
2 pkg. Equal, if desired

Mix in blender until smooth. Makes 2 servings.

Nutrients per serving:		Exchanges:	
Calories	207	Fruit	2
Fat	.75g	Milk	1
Cholesterol	2.5mg		
Carbohydrate	39.5g		
Sodium	60.5mg		

Extreme heat may cause diet sodas to lose their sweetness.

SUMMER'S DRINK

1 (2-qt. mix) pkg. sugar-free Kool-Aid (any flavor)
6 cups cold water
1 (6-oz.) can frozen orange juice (unsweetened)
2 (12-oz.) cans diet ginger ale

Mix Kool-Aid with 6 cups cold water in a large container. Make sure mix is dissolved. Add 1 (6-oz.) can frozen orange juice with 2 (12-oz.) cans diet ginger ale. Stir to dissolve the juice, then serve over ice. Yields 6 (8-oz.) servings, or 2½ qts. of drink.

Nutrients per serving:		Exchanges:	
Calories	50	Fruit	1
Fat	0		
Cholesterol	0		
Carbohydrate	13g		
Sodium	0		

Note: This is a near freebie. Enjoy!

CRANAPPLE PUNCH

3 cups cranapple juice
1 cup orange juice
1/4 cup lemon juice
4 pkg. Equal
1 Tbs. sugar
1 tsp. whole allspice
1 tsp. whole cloves
3 cinnamon sticks

Put everything but spices in a 10-cup percolator. Put the spices in the basket and perk. Serves 6.

Nutrients per serving:		Exchanges:	
Calories	56	Fruit	1
Fat	0		
Cholesterol	0		
Carbohydrate	14g		
Sodium	8mg		

HOT WASSAIL PUNCH

1 qt. unfiltered apple juice
1 pt. Ocean Spray low-calorie cranberry cocktail
1 cup unsweetened orange juice (reconstituted frozen)
1/4 cup lemon juice
1 Tbs. sugar
8 pkg. Equal
1 tsp. whole cloves
1 tsp. whole allspice
3 cinnamon sticks

Mix everything but the spices in a 10-cup percolator. Put the spices in the basket and perk. Serves 9.

Nutrients per serving:		Exchanges:	
Calories	46	Fruit	1
Fat	0		
Cholesterol	0		
Carbohydrate	14g		
Sodium	2mg		

Breads

ORANGE CINNAMON ROLLS

1 pkg. (8) refrigerated breadsticks
1 Tbs. melted margarine
1/4 cup raisins
1/4 cup chopped walnuts
1 Tbs. brown sugar
1/2 tsp. cinnamon
1 tsp. grated orange peel
12 pkg. Equal
1/4 tsp. vanilla
2 Tbs. orange juice

Unroll breadsticks and flatten slightly. Brush with melted margarine. Press raisins and walnut pieces into dough. Mix brown sugar and cinnamon and sprinkle over dough. Roll up each breadstick like a jelly roll. Pinch to seal and place in greased, 8-inch round cake pan. Bake at 340 degrees for 20–25 minutes or until light brown. Mix Equal, vanilla, and orange juice and drizzle over breadsticks while still warm.

Nutrients per serving:	
Calories	143
Fat	6g
Cholesterol	0
Carbohydrate	17g
Sodium	172mg

Exchanges:	
Bread	1
Fruit	1/4
Fat	1

RAISIN BRAN MUFFINS

1 egg beaten
3/4 cup skim milk or 1/4 c. dry milk plus 3/4 cup water
$1\frac{1}{2}$ cups flour
1 tsp. baking powder
1/4 cup sugar
1/2 tsp. salt substitute
1 tsp. cinnamon
1/2 tsp. nutmeg
1 raw apple or hard pear, peeled and diced (about 1 cup)
1 cup Raisin Bran flakes

Set oven to 350 degrees. Put cupcake papers in muffin tin. (Use double papers for microwave cooking.) Beat egg well, add milk, and mix. Sift together the flour, baking powder, sugar, salt substitute, cinnamon, and nutmeg into bowl with egg and milk. Add apple or pear and Raisin Bran and stir just until moistened. Fill muffin tin and put in preheated oven. Cook muffins 10–12 minutes. For microwave, do 3–6 at a time and microwave on high for 1 minute; rotate and microwave for another minute. If not done, microwave 1 minute more.

Note: These are good without butter or margarine. Each pat of butter or margarine will add 50 calories. For a more tender muffin, add 2–4 Tbs. oil. Each Tbs. oil adds 8 calories to every muffin.

Nutrients per serving:		Exchanges:	
Calories	87	Bread	1 1/3
Fat	1g	Fruit	1/2
Cholesterol	22mg		
Carbohydrate	28g		
Sodium	16mg		

APPLE CRANBERRY MUFFINS

1 1/2 cups flour
1 tsp. baking soda
1/4 cup sugar
1 tsp. cinnamon
1/3 cup salad oil
1 egg plus 2 egg whites
1 tsp. vanilla
12 pkg. Equal
3/4 cup fresh cranberries
3/4 cup diced apples
1/4 cup chopped walnuts or pecans

Heat oven to 350 degrees. Grease muffins pan or use cupcake papers. Sift flour, baking soda, sugar, Equal, and cinnamon together. Set aside.

Beat oil, eggs, and vanilla in large bowl. Add dry ingredients and mix well. Fold in cranberries, apples, and nuts.

Fill muffin tins 3/4 full and bake 20 minutes until golden brown. Makes 12 muffins.

Nutrients per muffin:		Exchanges:	
Calories	152	Bread	1
Fat	6.5g	Fruit	1/2
Cholesterol	21mg	Fat	1
Carbohydrate	20g		
Sodium	103mg		

MICROWAVE APPLESAUCE MUFFINS

Muffins:

2 cups Bisquick
1 cup applesauce (unsweetened)
1/2 cup raisins (optional)
1/3 cup packed brown sugar
1 egg

Topping:

Mix together:
2 pkg. Equal
2 tsp. cinnamon

Line each of 6 custard cups or microwave muffin cups with 2 paper liners.

Mix all muffin ingredients. Fill cups 1/2 full. Sprinkle with cinnamon-Equal mixture. Arrange muffins in a ring in oven. Microwave on high 2½ to 5½ minutes or until top springs back at touch. Remove muffins from cups to wire racks. Moist spots will dry during cooling. Yields 14 muffins.

Nutrients per muffin:	
Calories	116
Fat	2g
Cholesterol	24mg
Carbohydrate	19g
Sodium	9mg

Exchanges:	
Bread	1
Fruit	1/2
Fat	1/2

HINT OF FRUIT MUFFINS

2½ cups Fruit and Fibre cereal with nuts
1 cup skim milk (or 1/3 cup powdered dry milk and 1 cup water)
1 egg
1/3 cup vegetable oil
1 cup flour
1/4 cup sugar
1/8 tsp. salt
1 Tbs. baking powder

Mix the cereal and milk in a small bowl. Let sit for 3 minutes, then stir in egg and oil. Combine flour, sugar, salt, and baking powder. Add to cereal mixture, stirring just enough to moisten flour. Spoon the batter (will be thick) into 12 greased, 6-oz. glass custard cups or metal muffin cups. Fill 3/4 full. Additional cereal may be sprinkled over batter. Bake at 400 degrees for 20–25 minutes until brown. Makes 12 muffins.

Nutrients per muffin:		Exchanges:	
Calories	162	Bread	$1^1/_2$
Fat	7g	Fat	1
Cholesterol	23mg		
Carbohydrate	23g		
Sodium	177mg		

Note: This muffin is good for a snack as well as breakfast. It can also be frozen. When co-workers eat donuts, you will have a treat too.

POOR MAN'S BREADSTICKS

6 "Lite" hot dog buns
1 tsp. garlic powder
1/2 cup margarine, melted
1/4 cup Parmesan cheese
Poppy or sesame seed

Preheat oven to 450 degrees. Cut buns in half lengthwise. Cut lengthwise again to make sticks. Add garlic powder to margarine; dip breadsticks into it. Sprinkle with cheese and seeds. Place on cookie sheet and toast about 8 minutes. Makes 24 sticks.

Nutrients per stick:		Exchanges:	
Calories	59	Bread	1/3
Fat	4g	Fat	1
Cholesterol	0mg		
Carbohydrate	5g		
Sodium	106mg		

To test the potency of baking powder that has been on your shelf for some time (months), drop a teaspoonful in a cup of hot water. If it bubbles, it is still good.

PINEAPPLE CARROT RAISIN MUFFINS

1 egg plus 2 egg whites
1/4 cup safflower oil
1 tsp. vanilla
1/2 cup raisins
1/4 cup brown sugar
1/2 cup shredded carrots (about 1 large)
2 cups flour
2 tsp. baking powder
18 pkg. Equal
1/2 tsp. cinnamon
1/4 tsp. ground ginger
8-oz. can crushed pineapple in own juice

Beat eggs, then add oil and vanilla and mix well. Stir in raisins, brown sugar, and carrot. Sift dry ingredients into mixture. Mix until dry ingredients are moistened. Add pineapple. Spoon into greased muffin tins. Bake at 375 for 20 to 25 minutes. Makes 12 large muffins or 15 small. (Servings are figured for 12.)

Nutrients per serving:		Exchanges:	
Calories	182	Bread	1
Fat	6.5g	Fruit	1
Cholesterol	22mg	Fat	1
Carbohydrate	29g		
Sodium	69mg		

OAT BRAN MUFFINS

2 cups oat bran
2 tsp. Sweet 'N Low brown sugar
1/4 cup brown sugar, packed
2 tsp. baking powder
1/4 tsp. salt
1/4 cup raisins, optional
2 Tbs. margarine, softened
1 cup skim milk
1/4 cup water
2 egg whites, slightly beaten

Preheat oven to 350. Spray 12 muffin cups with vegetable oil spray or line with paper baking cups. Mix dry ingredients and raisins. (Mash all lumps in sugar and Sweet 'N Low.) Stir in soft butter, then add milk, water, and egg whites. Mix. Spoon into baking cups. (Batter is soupy; stir between spoonings.) Bake 15 to 20 minutes. Makes 12 muffins.

Nutrients per serving:		Exchanges:	
Calories	111	Bread	1
Fat	2.8g	Fat	1/2
Cholesterol	0		
Carbohydrate	16.8g		
Sodium	134mg		

Place a couple of bay leaves or a stick of spearmint gum (still wrapped) in the bag or box with flour, cornmeal, beans, rice, or other staples to keep the weevils at bay.

OATMEAL WITH BRAN MUFFINS

1 1/4 cups flour
1 Tbs. baking powder
1/2 tsp. salt
1/2 tsp. cinnamon
3 Tbs. sugar
3 Tbs. SugarTwin
1 cup raw quick oatmeal plus bran
1/2 cup raisins
***1/4 cup chopped pecans**
1 egg
1 cup skim milk or 1/3 cup dry milk plus 1 cup water
1/4 cup safflower oil

Sift flour, baking powder, salt, cinnamon, sugar, and SugarTwin into large bowl. Stir in oatmeal, raisins, and nuts.

In another bowl, beat egg; add milk and oil. Mix well. Add liquids to dry mixture and stir just until dry ingredients are moistened. Batter will be lumpy.

Fill greased muffin tin half to 3/4 full. Bake at 400 degrees for 20–25 minutes. For microwave, use double cupcake papers; bake 90 seconds on high, turn muffin pan halfway around, and cook another 90 seconds to 2 minutes. Muffins may not look brown on top but will feel firm to the touch. Makes 12 muffins.

* Omit pecans and save 15 calories.

Nutrients per serving:	
Calories	156
Fat	5.5g
Cholesterol	21mg
Carbohydrate	24g
Sodium	188mg

Exchanges:	
Breads	1
Fruit	1/2
Fat	1

OATMEAL-PUMPKIN BREAD

6 Tbs. margarine
1/4 cup sugar
3/4 cup SugarTwin
1 egg plus 2 egg whites
1 1/4 cups cooked mashed pumpkin
1/4 cup skim milk
1 tsp. cinnamon
1/2 tsp. nutmeg
2 cups biscuit mix
1 cup quick-cooking oatmeal
1/2 cup raisins or nuts

Cream margarine and sugars; beat in eggs. Stir in pumpkin, milk, and spices. In a separate bowl, combine biscuit mix, oatmeal and raisins. Add to pumpkin mixture and stir until moistened. Pour into greased 9 x 5 x 3-inch pan. Bake at 350 degrees for 45 minutes. Makes 1 loaf (16 slices).

Nutrients per serving:		Exchanges:	
Calories	91	Bread	1/2
Fat	4g	Fruit	1/4
Cholesterol	34mg	Fat	1
Carbohydrate	12g		
Sodium	197mg		

PUMPKIN NUT BREAD

1 cup pumpkin
3/4 cup SugarTwin
1/4 cup sugar
1/2 cup skim milk
1 egg plus 2 egg whites
2 cups sifted flour
2 tsp. baking powder
1/2 tsp. baking soda
1 tsp. cinnamon
1/2 tsp nutmeg
1/4 cup oil (safflower)
***1/3 cup raisins**
***1/3 cup chopped pecans**

Combine pumpkin, SugarTwin, sugar, milk, and eggs in mixing bowl. Sift dry ingredients together into bowl. Add oil; mix 'til well blended. Stir in nuts and raisins. Spread in well-greased 9 x 5 x 3-inch loaf pan. Bake in 350-degree oven for 45–55 minutes or until toothpick inserted in center comes out clean. Makes 1 loaf (12 slices).

Note: For 2 loaves use 1 can (No. 303) Libby's pumpkin and double remaining ingredients. Bread may be frozen.

* Omit raisins for 9 less calories.
* Omit pecans for 11 less calories and 1 gram less fat.

Nutrients per serving:		Exchanges:	
Calories	136	Bread	1
Fat	5g	Fruit	1/4
Cholesterol	16mg	Fat	1
Carbohydrate	19g		
Sodium	23.5mg		

BANANA BREAD

1/4 cup sugar
3/4 cup SugarTwin
1/3 cup margarine
1 egg plus 2 egg whites
1 tsp. baking soda
2 cups flour
4 Tbs. milk
3/4 tsp. vinegar
3 ripe bananas, mashed

Blend sugar, SugarTwin, and margarine. Add eggs and mix well. Sift flour and soda into bowl and stir. Mix milk and vinegar together, then add to mixture. Fold in bananas. Bake 1 hour at 350 degrees in greased 9 x 5 loaf pan. Let cool and cut into 20 slices.

Nutrients per slice:		Exchanges:	
Calories	108	Bread	1
Fat	3.6g	Fruit	1/4
Cholesterol	14mg	Fat	1
Carbohydrate	17g		
Sodium	63mg		

FRUITY NUT BREAD

3 cups pared, diced raw apple or hard pears (about 3)
1/2 cup water
1/4 cup brown sugar, packed
2 cups flour
1 tsp. baking powder
1 tsp. baking soda
1/4 tsp. salt
1 tsp. cinnamon
1/2 tsp. allspice
1/2 cup seedless raisins
1/4 cup walnuts or pecans, finely chopped
1 cup oatmeal, raw (quick or regular)
1 egg and 2 egg whites, beaten
1 ripe banana, mashed
1/4 cup cooking oil

Set oven at 350. Grease loaf pan and put 9 cupcake papers in muffin tin. Combine apples (or pears), water, and brown sugar in small saucepan and cook until apples are almost tender, about 5 minutes. Put apple mixture in refrigerator until it cools down. (If you mix hot ingredients with baking soda and liquid, it will start the leavening action before you get it in the oven and the muffins won't rise as much.)

Sift the flour, baking powder, baking soda, salt, cinnamon, and allspice together. Stir in raisins, nuts, and oatmeal. Add beaten eggs, mashed banana, and oil. Stir just until moistened. Add cooled apple and water mixture. Blend until just moistened.

Immediately fill 9 holes in muffin tin and loaf pan and put in preheated oven. Cook loaf 30–35 minutes (less for glass pan). Cook muffins 10–12 minutes. For microwave, use 2 cupcake papers per muffin; do 3–6 at a time and microwave on high for about 2 minutes.

This makes 1 loaf and 9 muffins, which are so good you may not even miss having butter on them. Serves 18.

Nutrients per serving:		Exchanges:	
Calories	154	Bread	1
Fat	5g	Fruit	1/2
Cholesterol	30mg	Fat	1
Carbohydrates	22g		
Sodium	44mg		

In recipes calling for 2 eggs, use 1 egg and 2 egg whites. You will eliminate 213 mg cholesterol, and even cakes turn out well.

SUGARLESS CRANBERRY-PECAN BREAD

- 2 cups sifted flour
- 1 tsp. baking soda
- 1 tsp. salt
- 1/2 tsp. cinnamon
- 1/2 tsp. nutmeg
- 1 egg
- Liquid sugar substitute to equal 1 cup sugar
- 1/3 cup orange juice
- 1 tsp. orange rinds
- 3 tsp. white vinegar plus enough water to make 1/2 cup
- 1/4 cup diet margarine (soft)
- 1 cup chopped cranberries
- 24 chopped pecans

Blend flour, baking soda, salt, cinnamon, and nutmeg in a large bowl. Beat egg; add sugar substitute, orange juice and rind, vinegar-water, and softened margarine. Combine egg and flour mixture and stir until moistened. Add cranberries and nuts and stir lightly. Fold batter into a nonstick pan or waxed paper-lined pan (8¼ x 4½ x 3-inch loaf pan). Bake at 350 degrees for 70 minutes. Makes 15 slices.

Note: This bread should be put in refrigerator overnight.

Nutrients per slice:		Exchanges:	
Calories	96	Bread	1
Fat	4g	Fat	1
Cholesterol	18mg		
Carbohydrate	14g		
Sodium	183mg		

ORANGE CRANBERRY NUT BREAD

2 Tbs. melted margarine
Juice of 1 orange
Grated rind of 1 orange
Boiling water
1 egg, beaten
1/4 cup brown sugar
2 cups flour
2 tsp. baking powder
18 pkg. Equal
1/2 cup raw cranberries, cut in half
1/3 cup chopped pecans

Melt the margarine in a microwave oven. Put orange juice and grated rind in a 1 cup measuring cup. Fill cup with boiling water. Add this slowly to beaten egg. Add melted margarine and mix. Fold in brown sugar, then combine sifted dry ingredients, cranberries and nuts and mix well. Batter will be thick. Spread in greased 9 x 5-inch loaf pan and bake in preheated oven at 325 for 1 hour to 1¼ hours. Let cool thoroughly before cutting into 12 generous slices.

Nutrients per serving:	
Calories	144
Fat	5g
Cholesterol	21mg
Carbohydrates	25g
Sodium	56mg

Exchanges:	
Bread	1½
Fruit	1/4
Fat	1

NUT BREAD

1¼ cups unsweetened applesauce
1 cup SugarTwin (48 pkg.)
1/2 cup Wesson oil
2 eggs
3 Tbs. 1/2 percent milk

* * *

2 cups sifted flour
1 tsp. baking soda
1/2 tsp. baking powder
1/2 tsp. cinnamon
1/4 tsp. salt
1/4 tsp. nutmeg
1/4 tsp. allspice
1/4 cup chopped pecans

Topping:

1/4 cup brown sugar
1/4 cup chopped pecans or raisins
1/2 tsp. cinnamon

Combine the first group and mix thoroughly. Sift the second group, withholding the nuts. Stir the two groups together; beat well. Fold in 1/2 cup nuts; turn into well-greased 9 x 5 x 3-inch loaf pan. Combine the topping and sprinkle over batter. Bake in moderate oven (350) for 1 hour or until done. Remove from pan; cool on rack. Makes 12 slices.

Nutrients per slice:		Exchanges:	
Calories	184	Bread	1
Fat	5g	Fruit	1
Cholesterol	22mg	Fat	1
Carbohydrate	28g		
Sodium	71mg		

ORANGE BRAN BREAD

- 1 cup unprocessed wheat bran
- 1 cup whole wheat flour
- 1 tsp. salt
- 1 tsp. baking soda
- 1 cup raisins
- 1 cup buttermilk
- 1 egg
- 1 can frozen orange juice (6 oz.)

Combine bran and wheat flour, salt, soda, and raisins. Combine buttermilk, egg, and orange juice, then put the mixtures together and stir until moistened. Turn into lightly greased and waxed paper-lined loaf pan. Bake at 350 degrees about 1 hour, until tester comes out clean. Bread does not rise and has dense texture similar to fruit cake. Makes 16 slices.

Nutrients per slice:		Exchanges:	
Calories	78	Bread	1
Fat	0	Fruit	1/2
Cholesterol	17mg		
Carbohydrate	17g		
Sodium	48mg		

SCRUMPTIOUS APPLE COFFEECAKE

Batter:

1 egg plus 2 egg whites
1 cup skim milk
1½ cups flour
1/2 tsp. salt
1 tsp. sugar

Fruit topping:

18 pkg. Equal
4 tsp. sugar
2 tsp. cinnamon
1/4 cup (1/2 stick) margarine, melted
3 large apples (Golden Delicious work well)

Mix Equal, sugar, and cinnamon. Melt margarine in frying pan over medium heat. Slice apples (peel if skin is bitter or tough) 1/8" thick and mix with 3 tsp. of cinnamon mixture.

Stir 3 tsp. cinnamon mixture into melted margarine. Add apples to pan, and stir until apples are well coated. Remove from heat while making batter.

Pour apple mixture into 10-inch ceramic or glass pie plate. (Works okay in metal tin, but glass takes less time to cook.)

To make batter: beat eggs and stir in milk; sift flour, salt, and 1 tsp. sugar into egg and milk mixture; and beat until smooth.

Pour over apple mixture and sprinkle remaining cinnamon sugar mixture over top. Bake about 20 minutes at 400. Serve immediately. Makes 6 servings.

Banana Classic Coffeecake: Make the same as above except use 2 large bananas.

Nutrients per serving:	Apple	Banana	Exchanges:	
Calories	291	186	Bread	1½
Fat	6.2g	6.2g	Fruit	½
Cholesterol	33mg	33mg	Fat	1
Carbohydrate	31.5g	31.5g		
Sodium	183mg	137.5g		

Use diet margarine with half the calories of regular margarine.

CRANBERRY BUNS

- 1 cup fresh cranberries
- 1/4 cup sugar
- 1/4 cup SugarTwin
- 1 tsp. grated orange peel
- 2 tsp. lemon juice
- 1 large egg, beaten
- 2/3 cup buttermilk (or 2/3 cup skim milk plus 1 Tbs. vinegar)
- 3 cups flour
- 3 tsp. baking powder
- 1 tsp. baking soda
- 1/4 tsp. salt
- 1/3 cup margarine

Set oven at 375 degrees. Combine cranberries, sugar, SugarTwin, orange peel, and lemon juice in a small bowl. Beat egg in large bowl and mix in buttermilk (or skim milk and vinegar). Add cranberry mixture. Sift dry ingredients into this and stir just until moistened. If dough is too sticky to make into a ball, sprinkle with flour. Knead dough on floured surface 5 or 6 times until it sticks together well. Roll into balls (about 13) and place on greased cookie sheet. Bake 15–20 minutes or until golden brown.

Nutrients per serving:		Exchanges:	
Calories	195	Bread	$1\frac{1}{2}$
Fat	6g	Fruit	1/4
Cholesterol	20mg	Fat	1
Carbohydrate	31		
Sodium	206mg with buttermilk, or 199 with skim milk		

GRANDMOTHER'S INDIAN CORN CAKE

- $1\frac{1}{2}$ cups skim milk
- $1\frac{1}{2}$ cups yellow cornmeal
- 2 Tbs. molasses
- 1/2 cup cooked pumpkin
- 1/4 cup flour
- 2 tsp. baking powder
- 1/4 tsp. ginger
- 1/8 tsp. ground cloves
- 1/2 tsp. cinnamon
- 1/4 cup margarine

Scald milk and pour slowly over the cornmeal. Stir in the pumpkin and molasses and set aside to cool. Sift in flour, baking powder, and spices. Melt margarine, and pour slowly into batter. Stir until well mixed. Pour into greased 8-inch square cake pan. Bake for 30 minutes at 350 degrees. Yields 12 servings.

Nutrients per serving:		Exchanges:	
Calories	117	Bread	1 1/4
Fat	3.7g	Fat	1
Cholesterol	3mg		
Carbohydrate	17g		
Sodium	41mg		

Keep powdered milk on hand for cooking and baking. It's cheaper and has less calories.

SOUTHERN CORNBREAD

1 cup yellow cornmeal
1 cup flour
4 tsp. baking powder
3/4 tsp. salt substitute
1 medium egg, slightly beaten
1 cup skim milk

Sift dry ingredients together. Add egg and milk; mix well. Pour into 12 x 8-inch pan which has been sprayed with a nonstick vegetable coating. Bake at 425 for 25 minutes. Cut into 12 equal squares.

Nutrients per serving:		Exchanges:	
Calories	81	Bread	1
Fat	1g		
Cholesterol	0		
Carbohydrate	15g		
Sodium	142mg		

CAROLYN'S YANKEE CORNBREAD

1 cup flour
1/2 tsp. salt
4 tsp. baking powder (use double-action type)
3 Tbs. sugar
1/2 cup yellow cornmeal
1 egg white
1 cup plus 2 Tbs. skim milk
2 Tbs. Fleishmann's corn oil margarine, melted

Sift flour, salt, baking powder, sugar, and cornmeal into a bowl. Add egg white and milk. Mix quickly, but do not beat. Pour in melted margarine and stir. Pour batter into well-greased 9 x 9-inch square baking pan and bake at 400 degrees for 20–25 minutes. Cut into 16 squares and serve hot.

Nutrients per serving:		Exchanges:	
Calories	74	Bread	1
Fat	1.5g		
Cholesterol	.3mg		
Carbohydrate	10g		
Sodium	178mg		

Note: Add 50 calories per pat of margarine or butter used.

Desserts

Sweeteners

1 Tbs.	Calories	1 Tbs.	Calories
Honey	65	Fructose	45
Table syrup (corn, maple)	61	Sucrose	45
Brown sugar	52	Molasses (cane, blackstrap)	43
Refined table sugar	45	Powdered sugar	25

Don't be fooled. This list is ALL SUGAR;
only the names are different.

CAROLYN'S LIGHT CHEESECAKE

Crust:

1 (3-oz.) pkg. sugar-free Jell-o (lemon, lime, or strawberry)
1 cup boiling water
1 cup graham cracker crumbs (12 squares, save 1/4 cup to sprinkle on top)
3 Tbs. melted margarine
1 large can cold evaporated milk

Filling:

8 oz. Neufchatel cheese or lite cream cheese
1/4 cup sugar
18 pkg. Equal
2 tsp. vanilla extract
1/2 tsp. almond flavoring (omit vanilla and almond flavoring with strawberry Jell-o)

Dissolve Jell-o in boiling water; cool in the refrigerator. Mix the crumbs and melted margarine. Save 1/4 cup of crumbs to sprinkle on top. Press mixture in bottom of 8 x 11 or 9 x 9 pan and chill crust.

Whip milk until thick. (If it won't whip, add 1/2 tsp. lemon juice and try again.) Put whipped milk in refrigerator.

Mix the cream cheese, sugar, Equal, and flavorings. (Whip milk again if needed.) Add the Jell-o mixture gradually. Mix well. Gradually fold whipped evaporated milk into the Jell-o mixture, then whip again for about 30 seconds. Pour into crust.

Sprinkle reserved crumbs on top. Chill 6 hours or longer. Crust is not very firm, so be careful when serving. Serves 12.

Nutrients per serving:		Exchanges:	
Calories	166	Bread	1
Fat	10g	Milk	1/2
Cholesterol	39mg	Fat	2
Carbohydrate	13g		
Sodium	188mg		

FROZEN LOW-CALORIE CHEESECAKE
(An even lighter cheesecake)

Use the same method as above, but:

1. Use skimmed, evaporated milk instead of regular evaporated milk.
2. Use only 3 Tbs. melted margarine instead of 4. Crust will be crumbly, so be careful when you serve it.
3. Freeze 2 hours or until solid. Take out of the freezer 10–30 minutes before serving. Serves 12.

Nutrients per serving:		Exchanges:	
Calories	148	Bread	1
Fat	8g	Milk	1/2
Cholesterol	19mg	Fat	2
Carbohydrate	14g		
Sodium	207mg		

MICROWAVE STRAWBERRY CHEESECAKE

2 Tbs. margarine
2/3 cup graham cracker crumbs (9 squares)
1 lb. frozen strawberries (with no sugar added)
1 (8-oz.) pkg. light cream cheese (Neufchatel or light)
2 large eggs
15 pkg. Equal
2 Tbs.cornstarch
1 (15–16 oz.) carton part

Microwave the margarine in an 8-inch round baking dish or 8-inch square Corningware dish on high for 40 seconds or until melted. Add crumbs and mix. Press firmly to cover bottom of dish. Set aside half of the strawberries for the topping. Put the rest of the strawberries in blender with half of the cream cheese and 2 eggs. Blend and add the rest of the cream cheese. Add 12 pkg. Equal, 1 Tbs. cornstarch, and 1 carton ricotta cheese. Blend until all is smooth. Pour filling over crust. Microwave on medium-high (or 70 percent) for 3 minutes and rotate 1/4 turn. Repeat 3 or 4 more times until center only jiggles slightly. Let cool and refrigerate.

Add 2 Tbs. of water to 1 Tbs. cornstarch in a small saucepan. Stir until blended, then add rest of strawberries. Cook over medium heat, stirring and watching constantly until strawberries are thickened. Let cool and mix in 3 pkg. Equal. Refrigerate.

When topping and cheesecake are both chilled, spread strawberry topping over cheesecake. Serves 10.

Nutrients per serving:		Exchanges:	
Calories	194	Meat (cheese)	2
Fat	12.5g	Fruit	1/2
Cholesterol	76.6mg	Fat	1
Carbohydrate	5g		
Sodium	207mg		

Kitchen Tips

1 Tbs. pumpkin pie spice = 2 tsp. cinnamon, 1/2 tsp. ginger, 1/2 tsp. cloves, 1/2 tsp. nutmeg.

Substitute 3 Tbs. cocoa for 1 square of unsweetened chocolate.

Substitute for whipped cream: Beat a banana and the white of one egg together until stiff.

Most artificial sweeteners break down when boiled more than a few minutes.

DIET APPLE PIE

- 1 (6-oz.) can frozen apple juice, unsweetened
- 1 tsp. cinnamon
- 2 Tbs. flour
- 3–4 apples, sliced

Mix all but the apples. Put apples in 9-inch pie crust and pour mixture over apples. Bake at 350 until golden brown. Serves 8. (Submitted by Gladys Hayes.)

Nutrients per serving:		Exchanges:	
Calories	179	Fat	1/2
Fat	7g	Fruit	1
Cholesterol	0mg	Bread	1
Carbohydrate	27g		
Sodium	138mg		

QUICK APPLE PIE

9-inch graham cracker pie crust:

12 graham cracker squares, crushed
4 Tbs. Fleischmann's margarine, melted

Filling:

3–4 medium-sized apples, chopped
1 (6-oz.) can frozen unsweetened apple juice
1 tsp. cinnamon
2 Tbs. flour
Dash nutmeg
4 pkg. Equal
2 Tbs. raisins (optional)

Line 9-inch pie crust with chopped apples. Mix remaining ingredients and pour over apples. Cook at 375 degrees until crust is golden brown. Serves 8. (Submitted by Gladys Hayes.)

Nutrients per serving:		Exchanges:	
Calories	176	Bread	1
Fat	40g	Fruit	1
Cholesterol	0mg		
Carbohydrate	26g		
Sodium	71mg		

Quick sherbet: Prepare diet Jell-o as directed on package and freeze. When solid, put in blender or beat with electric mixer.

BAKED APPLE

1 med. apple
1 pkg. Equal
1/8 tsp. cinnamon
1 Tbs. water

Peel and quarter apple. Cut out seedy section. Cut each quarter into 2 lengthwise. Place on microwave-safe plate. Sprinkle apple sections with cinnamon and Equal. Pour 1 Tbs. water into bottom of plate. Cook on high for five minutes. For more than 1 serving, you may have to increase time.

Nutrients per serving:		Exchanges:	
Calories	80	Fruit	1½
Fat	0		
Cholesterol	0		
Carbohydrate	21g		
Sodium	—		

MICROWAVE SWEET SUGARLESS APPLE PIE

1 can (12-oz.) unsweetened frozen apple juice, thawed
3 tsp. cornstarch
1/4 tsp. salt
1 tsp. ground cinnamon
1/2 tsp. ground nutmeg
5–6 large golden apples, peeled and sliced 1/4-inch thick (6 cups)
2 tsp. firm margarine
9-inch baked shell (1½-inch deep dish)

Stir in a 2 qt. bowl the apple juice, cornstarch, salt, cinnamon, nutmeg and mix well. Add apples. Cut margarine into small pieces to dot apples. Cover with wax paper. Microwave on high for 8 minutes. Stir at 4 minutes.

Uncover and microwave for second 8 minutes. Again stir after 4 minutes. Apple slices should be fork tender. Cool 30 minutes before spooning apples into the baked pie shell. Refrigerate before serving. Serves 8.

Nutrients per serving:		Exchanges:	
Calories	233	Bread	1
Fat	9g	Fruit	2
Cholesterol	0mg		
Carbohydrate	38g		
Sodium	174mg		

For fewer calories and fats in recipes, use Neufchatel rather than regular cream cheese.

SPICY APPLE TWISTS

1 1/2 cups flour
1/2 tsp. salt
1/3 cup cold margarine (made with vegetable oil)
1 Tbs. margarine, melted
7 Tbs. cold water
2 large apples
4 tsp. sugar
1 1/2 tsp. cinnamon
1 tsp. nutmeg
3/4 cup water

Mix flour with salt and cut in cold margarine with a pastry blender or use two knives, cutting criss-cross. Sprinkle in cold water and mix with a fork until dough holds together. Squeeze together with hands and roll out on floured surface. Be sure to flour rolling pin often or dough will stick. Roll into a rectangle and cut into 16 strips 1-inch wide and 10 inches long.

Peel apples and cut each into 8 wedges. Cut out the hard core center. Wrap a strip of dough around each wedge and squeeze gently so dough will stay on apple. Place in a 13 x 9 x 2-inch pan. Brush with melted margarine and sprinkle with mixture of sugar, cinnamon, and nutmeg. Pour 3/4 cup water into the pan around the bottom of the pastries. Bake in 400-degree oven 20–30 minutes until golden brown. Serves 5 (3 wedges each).

Nutrients per serving:		Exchanges:	
Calories	305	Bread	2
Fat	13g	Fruit	1/2
Cholesterol	0	Fat	2 1/2
Carbohydrate	41g		
Sodium	498mg		

Compare with 1/6 of a regular 9-inch apple pie, made with vegetable shortening:

Nutrients per serving:		Exchanges:	
Calories	405	Bread	3
Fat	18g	Fruit	1
Cholesterol	60mg	Fat	3 1/2
Carbohydrate	60g		
Sodium	369mg		

APRICOT CUSTARD PIE

1 jar (7 1/2 oz.) junior apricots with tapioca
2 whole eggs and 4 egg whites
1/3 cup sugar
1 1/2 tsp. vanilla
1/2 to 1 tsp. grated lemon peel
1/4 tsp. salt substitute
1/4 tsp. ground ginger
1 1/2 cups very hot milk
1 9-inch pie shell, unbaked

In medium saucepan, mix together apricots, eggs, sugar, vanilla, lemon peel, salt substitute, and ginger until well blended. Add milk gradually. Cook, stirring, until thick. Pour into pie shell. Bake in 400-degree oven 25 minutes or until knife inserted near center comes out clean. Cool on wire rack. Serves 8.

Nutrients per serving:	
Calories	247
Fat	8.5g
Cholesterol	72mg
Carbohydrate	28g
Sodium	237mg

Exchanges:	
Bread	1 1/2
Meat (eggs)	1/2
Fruit	1/2
Fat	1 1/2

OUR LEMON PIE

3 Tbs. margarine
10 graham cracker squares
1/2 cup cold skimmed evaporated milk
1 envelope Dream Whip
27 pkg. Equal
2 egg yolks
Juice of 2 large lemons (1/2 cup juice)
3 egg whites
3 Tbs. sugar

Melt margarine on medium to low heat. Roll graham crackers into crumbs with rolling pin. Mix crumbs and melted margarine. Pat to make crust on bottom and sides of pie pan. Chill.

Add cold evaporated milk to Dream Whip (do not add vanilla). Sprinkle in 24 pkg. Equal. Mix and beat according to directions. Beat egg yolks slightly, and gradually stir in lemon juice. Gradually fold in the whipped Dream Whip. Spread in pie crust. Turn on broiler so it will get hot. Beat 3 egg whites frothy (use clean beaters so whites will beat up as fluffy as possible). Add 1 Tbs. sugar and beat until blended in. Add another Tbs. sugar and 3 Equal pkg. and beat until soft peaks form. Spread meringue over top.

Spread meringue to stick to the edges so it won't shrink when you broil it. Put under broiler for 30–60 seconds until meringue is lightly browned. IT DOESN'T TAKE LONG AT ALL AND IS EASY TO BURN. The flavors will blend better if you chill for 5 hours. Serves 8.

Nutrients per serving:		Exchanges:	
Calories	144	Bread	1
Fat	5g	Fruit	1/2
Cholesterol	.6mg	Milk	1/2
Carbohydrate	27g	Fat	1
Sodium	81mg		

KEY LIME PUDDING AND PIE

Crust:

12 graham cracker squares

1/4 cup margarine, melted

Filling:

1 egg

1 pkg. diet Jell-o vanilla instant pudding

16-oz. Dannon Lowfat Yogurt (other brands have more calories)

25 pkg. Equal

2 Tbs. sugar

Juice of 2 limes

Crust: Crush 12 graham cracker squares; mix with 1/4 cup margarine, melted. Press into 8- or 9-inch pie pan.

Filling: Beat the egg. Stir in pudding, yogurt, Equal, sugar, and lime juice. Chill 4 hours. Serve without crust if desired. Serves 8.

Nutrients per serving:	*Pudding*	*w/Crust*
Calories	183	278
Fat	7g	16g
Cholesterol	36mg	36mg
Carbohydrate	17g	13g
Sodium	268mg	332mg

Exchanges:	*Pudding*	*Pie*
Bread	0	1/2
Milk	1	1
Fruit	1/2	1/2
Fat	1	3

VICKI'S PINEAPPLE FROSTY

4 sliced bananas
12 oz. frozen natural pineapple juice
4 Tbs. coconut
1 cup lowfat yogurt

Blend 2 bananas with juice and coconut. Add rest of banana and blend. Stir in yogurt. Freeze. Makes 8 servings. (From Vicki Harrold.)

Nutrients per serving:		Exchanges:	
Calories	93	Milk	1/4
Fat	1.5g	Fruit	$1\frac{1}{2}$
Cholesterol	0		
Carbohydrate	25g		
Sodium	18mg		

Dunk whole citrus fruits in boiling water before squeezing to get more juice.

LIME PARFAIT

1 can (13-oz.) evaporated skim milk
2 tsp. vanilla extract
2 envelopes unflavored gelatin
1/3 cup lime juice
1 cup boiling water
18 pkg. Equal
Zest of 3 limes (colored part of grated rind)
1 lime, thinly sliced

Combine milk and vanilla. Freeze about 30 minutes. Meanwhile, in blender or food processor, combine gelatin and lime juice. Let stand about 1 minute. Add boiling water and Equal. Blend until smooth. Chill until slightly thickened (about 45 minutes). Whip frozen milk until stiff. Fold in lime zest. Gradually blend gelatin mix into whipped milk and mix well.

Spoon into parfait glasses. Chill until set. Garnish with lime zest and lime slice. Makes 8 servings of 1 cup each.

Nutrients per serving:		Exchanges:	
Calories	84	Milk	1/2
Fat	0	Fruit	1/2
Cholesterol	1mg		
Carbohydrate	10g		
Sodium	37mg		

BLACK FOREST PARFAIT

3 oz. Neufchatel cream cheese
2 cups cold skim milk
1 3-oz. pkg. Jell-o sugar-free instant chocolate pudding mix
1 Tbs. cornstarch
1/3 cup cherry juice
1 can (1 lb.) red sour pitted cherries (water packed)
6 pkg. Equal

Blend cream cheese with 1/4 cup skim milk on low speed of electric mixer, until smooth. Add remaining milk and pudding mix. Mix 1 or 2 minutes or until smooth.

Mix cornstarch in cherry juice until dissolved. Add to cherries and cook until it boils for 1 minute. Remove from heat and stir in Equal.

Alternately spoon pudding and cherries into parfait dishes, ending with pudding. Garnish with 2 cherries. Yields 6 servings.

Nutrients per serving:		Exchanges:	
Calories	116	Bread	1/2
Fat	3.5g	Milk	1/2
Cholesterol	14mg	Fruit	1/2
Carbohydrate	16g	Fat	1
Sodium	304		

SUNSHINE ORANGE PUDDING

1 (3-oz.) pkg. sugar-free gelatin (any flavor)
3/4 cup boiling water
1/2 cup cold orange juice
6–8 ice cubes
1½ cups diced orange sections (can be canned)

Dissolve gelatin in boiling water. Mix orange juice and enough ice to make 1¼ cups. Pour into gelatin and stir until it becomes slightly thickened. Remove any ice cubes not melted. Add oranges. Pour into fancy dessert dishes. Chill at least 30 minutes. Yield 6 servings.

Nutrients per serving:		Exchanges:	
Calories	— (trace)	Fruit	—
Fat	—		
Cholesterol	—		
Carbohydrate	—		
Sodium	—		

STRAWBERRIES ROMANOFF

1/4 cup lowfat yogurt per serving (put in custard cup)
4–5 pkg. Equal per serving
4 fresh or thawed frozen strawberries per serving
Dash of nutmeg

For each serving, mix yogurt with Equal and a dash of nutmeg. Then add strawberries and stir. Serves 1.

Nutrients per serving:		Exchanges:	
Calories	57	Milk	1/2
Fat	1g	Fruit	1/3
Cholesterol	0mg		
Carbohydrate	5g		
Sodium	40mg		

BANANA PUDDING

1 lg. pkg. sugar-free instant vanilla pudding (any brand)
2 cups skim milk
1 banana, mashed

Mix according to directions. Add banana. Spoon into six 1/4-cup containers.

Nutrients per serving:		Exchanges:	
Calories	99	Fruit	1/3
Fat	0g	Milk	1/3
Cholesterol	2mg	Bread	1
Carbohydrate	19g		
Sodium	243mg		

BANANA TAPIOCA PUDDING

3 Tbs. sugar
3 Tbs. Equal
3 Tbs. Minute Tapioca
2 3/4 cups skim milk
1 egg, slightly beaten
1 tsp. vanilla
1 banana, chopped
Dollop Cool Whip

Follow directions on tapioca box, substituting 3 Tbs. sugar and 3 Tbs. Equal for the sugar. Remove from heat. Add vanilla and 1 chopped banana. Chill. Serve with dollop of whipped topping. Serves 6.

Nutrients per serving:		Exchanges:	
Calories	136	Milk	1
Fat	2g	Fat	1
Cholesterol	3mg		
Carbohydrate	1g		
Sodium	71mg		

TWO-WAY BREAD PUDDING

- 1 cup raisins or dates
- 4 cups bread cubes
- 1 whole egg
- 3 egg whites
- 1½ tsp. vanilla
- 3 Tbs. brown sugar
- 1 qt. skim milk

Mix raisins or dates in with bread cubes in a 9 x 9-inch baking pan coated with vegetable spray. Beat the egg and egg whites slightly. Mix in vanilla, sugar, milk. Stir until sugar is dissolved. Pour mixture over bread cubes and bake at 375 for 45 to 55 minutes, or until a knife poked near the center comes out clean. Serves 9–10.

Nutrients per serving:	*Raisins*	*Dates*	Exchanges:	*Raisins*	*Dates*
Calories	144	150	Bread	1	1
Fat	2g	2g	Fruit	1	2
Cholesterol	30mg	30mg			
Carbohydrate	28g	26g			
Sodium	98mg	97mg			

Lessen the need for sugar in desserts by sweetening with fruits.

PEACH TAPIOCA

- 3 Tbs. tapioca (not pearl type)
- 2¾ cups skim milk
- 1 egg, separated
- 8 pkg. Equal
- 1 tsp. vanilla
- 2 Tbs. sugar
- 1 cup frozen peaches or peaches canned in water or own juice

Mix tapioca with 2 Tbs. of the milk. Add egg yolk and mix well. Stir in rest of the milk and the Equal. Let stand 5 minutes. Cook over medium heat, stirring often until mixture boils for 1 minute. Take off heat and add vanilla. Beat egg white with mixer until foamy. Add 1 Tbs. sugar and beat well before adding second Tbs. and beating some more. Beat until egg white stands in soft peaks. Slowly pour a thin stream of hot tapioca into egg white as you fold it in with a rubber spatula. Serve warm or cold. Makes 6 servings.

Nutrients per serving:		Exchanges:	
Calories	174	Bread	1
Fat	2g	Fruit	1/2
Cholesterol	48mg		
Carbohydrate	18g		
Sodium	71mg		

FROZEN FRUIT FUN DESSERT

- 1 pkg. frozen unsweetened raspberries (16 oz. = about 2 cups)
- 1 cup reconstructed frozen orange juice
- 24 pkg. Equal
- 1/2 cup dry nonfat milk
- 1/2 cup ice water
- 2 Tbs. lemon juice

Purée raspberries (about 2 cups). Strain to remove seeds, then place in large bowl. Add orange juice and sweetener.

In another large mixing bowl, combine dry nonfat milk, ice water, and lemon juice. Beat on high until stiff, about 6 minutes. Slowly add fruit mixture and stir gently. Spoon into freezer-safe dessert dishes.

Leftover raspberry mix can be put into 3-oz. paper cups with ice cream sticks or plastic spoons for handles. Freeze overnight. Desserts can be set out as you sit down to eat your meal. Children will love eating dessert on a stick. Serves 8.

Note: Can use other fruits — strawberries, ripe bananas, or peaches.

Nutrients per serving:		Exchanges:	
Calories	47	Fruit	1/2
Fat	0g		
Cholesterol	1mg		
Carbohydrate	7g		
Sodium	9mg		

DELIGHTFULLY TROPICAL

1 (3-oz.) pkg. strawberry/ banana gelatin (sugar-free)
3/4 cup boiling water
1/2 cup pineapple juice
Ice cubes
1 cup cold skim milk
1 Tbs. flaked coconut (optional)

Dissolve gelatin in boiling water. Combine 1/2 cup of juice and enough ice cubes to make 1 cup. Add to gelatin and stir until ice is completely melted. Add milk and blend. Pour into dessert dishes and chill until set (at least 30 minutes). Garnish with sprinkle of flaked coconut if desired. Makes 5 servings.

Note: May use any flavor red gelatin.

Nutrients per serving:		Exchanges:	
Calories	31	Milk	1/2
Fat	0		
Cholesterol	.8mg		
Carbohydrate	6g		
Sodium	25mg		

AMBROSIA

2 oranges
2 bananas
2 pkg. Equal
1/3 cup coconut

Peel and slice an orange. Then cut slices into halves or quarters. Add sliced bananas, Equal, and coconut and mix well. Let stand covered in refrigerator for half an hour. Serves 4.

Nutrients per serving:		Exchanges:	
Calories	107	Fruit	1 1/2
Fat	3mg		
Cholesterol	0		
Carbohydrate	22g		
Sodium	1mg		

When you have egg yolk or fat on beaters that you use for whipping egg whites, the whites will not beat up as fluffy.

Eggs separate more easily when cold, but make better volume when beaten at room temperature. Separate 30 minutes before whipping.

APPLESAUCE DELIGHT

2 cups applesauce
1/2 tsp. ground cinnamon
1/2 tsp. nutmeg
1/3 cup raisins
1/4 cup chopped pecans
Dollop whipped topping

In small saucepan, combine all ingredients but whipped topping. Cook over medium heat until hot, stirring occasionally. Spoon into dessert dishes. Garnish with dollop of whipped topping if desired. Serve hot or cold. Makes 4 servings.

Nutrients per serving:		Exchanges:	
Calories	157	Fruit	1½
Fat	9g		
Cholesterol	0mg		
Carbohydrate	19g		
Sodium	3mg		

SPICED TEA CAKES

1/2 cup Fleischmann's margarine
1 egg
2 tsp. Sweet 'N Low (8 pkg.)
1¾ cups sifted flour
1 tsp. baking soda
1/4 tsp. salt
1 tsp. cinnamon
1/2 tsp. nutmeg
1/4 tsp. each, cloves, allspice, ginger
1 cup unsweetened applesauce
2 tsp. vanilla
1/3 cup raisins
1/3 cup chopped walnuts

Cream margarine until fluffy. Add beaten egg and Sweet 'N Low until light yellow. Sift dry ingredients together. Add to margarine mixture alternately with applesauce, blending well after each addition. Add vanilla; stir in raisins and nuts.

Preheat oven to 375 degrees. Line tea-cake pan with paper liners. Pour batter in 2/3 full and bake 15 to 20 minutes. If paper cups are not used, spray the cupcake pan with vegetable spray. Makes approximately 30 cakes.

Nutrients per serving:		Exchanges:	
Calories	61	Bread	1/2
Fat	5g	Fruit	1/4
Cholesterol	9mg		
Carbohydrate	6g		
Sodium	146mg		

The thinner and slicker the skin on citrus fruits, the more juice they contain.

CONSCIENCE-FREE CARROT CAKE

1/4 cup sugar
18 pkg. Equal
*1/2 cup plus 2 Tbs. safflower oil
$1\frac{1}{2}$ cups flour
$1\frac{1}{2}$ tsp. baking powder
1/2 tsp. salt
1 tsp. cinnamon
1/2 tsp. ground cloves
1 egg
3 egg whites
1/2 cup raisins
1 cup finely grated carrots
1/4 cup water
**1/4 cup chopped almonds or pecans

Glaze:
Juice and rind of 1 orange
6 pkg. Equal

Mix sugar, Equal, and oil in a large bowl. Sift into that the flour, baking powder, salt, cinnamon, and cloves. Add whole egg and beat with electric mixer until well blended. Add 3 egg whites and mix. Add carrots, raisins, water, and nuts. Beat on medium speed until well mixed.

Grease and flour a 9-inch Bundt pan. Pour batter in and bake at 350 for 30 to 35 minutes or until a toothpick inserted into the middle comes out clean. Cool in pan 10 to 15 minutes. Serves 16.

Optional glaze: Mix juice and grated rind of 1 orange with 6 pkg. Equal and pour over hot cake after removing from pan, which adds 7 calories per serving.

* You may use corn, soybean or sunflower oil, which have no cholesterol, but the cake might taste different.

** Adding 1/4 cup chopped almonds or pecans will add 12 calories and 1 g. fat to each serving, making fat exchanges 3 instead of $2\frac{1}{2}$.

Nutrients per serving:		Exchanges:	
Calories	176	Bread	1
Fat	12g	Fruit	1/2
Cholesterol	16mg	Fat	2 1/2
Carbohydrate	18g		
Sodium	148mg		

Carrot cake made the usual way has the following nutrients per serving.

Nutrients per serving for regular carrot cake:		Exchanges:	
Calories	485	Bread	2
Fat	25g	Fruit	2
Cholesterol	16mg	Fat	5
Carbohydrate	18g		
Sodium	461mg		

CHOCOLATE ROLL

Cake:

4 eggs, separated
1/2 tsp. cream of tartar
*3 Tbs. SugarTwin
3/4 cup skim milk
2 tsp. vanilla
1/4 tsp. almond flavoring
3/4 cup flour
1/3 cup cocoa
1 tsp. baking powder
1/2 tsp. baking soda
1/4 tsp. salt

Filling:

2/3 cup non-dairy cream powder
1/3 cup 2% milk
*3 pkg. Equal (or 2 Tbs. SugarTwin)
1/2 tsp. vanilla
1/2 tsp. almond flavoring

Spray pan with vegetable spray or grease well and lightly flour 10 x 15-inch pan. Beat egg whites and cream of tartar until foamy. Add 2 Tbs. of the SugarTwin and beat until mixture forms stiff peaks. (If you beat yolks first, wash beater thoroughly or the whites won't beat up as well.)

Beat yolks until they are thick and lemon-colored. Mix in milk and flavorings. Add dry ingredients, including the rest of the SugarTwin, and mix at low speed until moistened. Beat on medium speed for 2 minutes. Pour yolk mixture over whites and fold in carefully with a rubber spatula. Pour into pan and bake 7 minutes at 375 degrees.

Lightly flour a cotton dish towel. When the cake is done, remove from oven and let sit for 1 minute. Then loosen cake around the edges and turn out onto the floured towel. Starting with the short end, roll the cake up with the towel. Make sure the end of the cake is on the bottom so cake won't unroll while it's cooling. Let cool on a cake rack.

Unroll cooled cake and spread with filling to 1/2 inch from the edges. Save some for the top. Roll up cake and spread saved filling on top. Chill until time to serve. Cut into twelve 1/2-inch slices.

* SugarTwin works better in baked products, but Equal tastes better in mixtures that won't be cooked.

Nutrients per serving:		Exchanges:	
Calories	103	Bread	1
Fat	6g	Fat	1
Cholesterol	92mg		
Carbohydrate	12g		
Sodium	74mg		

Cake and cookie batter won't clump up on your mixer beaters if you spray non-stick vegetable spray on them before starting.

BANANA OATMEAL COOKIES

- 1/2 cup egg whites (about 4)
- 1/4 cup brown sugar
- 1/4 cup SugarTwin
- 1/2 cup raisins
- 1 ripe banana
- 1/3 cup vegetable oil (sunflower, safflower)
- 1/2 cup skim milk
- 1½ tsp. vanilla
- 1 cup whole wheat flour
- 1/2 tsp. baking soda
- 1/4 tsp. salt
- 1/2 tsp. cinnamon
- 1/4 tsp. nutmeg
- 1/4 tsp. cloves
- 1½ cups quick cooking oatmeal

Beat egg whites slightly in large bowl. Add brown sugar, SugarTwin, raisins, mashed banana, oil, milk, and vanilla. Mix well. Sift rest of dry ingredients except oatmeal into mixture and stir in. (If the last of the whole wheat flour is too coarse to go through sifter, just sprinkle what is left over the rest in the bowl.) Add oatmeal. Mix well. Drop by teaspoonfuls onto greased cookie sheets. Bake at 350 for 11 to 13 minutes. *After baking,* if sweeter cookie is desired, sprinkle 12–15 hot cookies with 1 packet of Sweet 'N Low or Equal or use real sugar for members of the family not on diet. Yield 46 cookies (2 cookies per serving).

Nutrients per serving:		Exchanges:	
Calories	91	Bread	1
Fat	3g	Fruit	1/4
Cholesterol	0	Fat	1/2
Carbohydrate	13g		
Sodium	101mg		

CINNAMON RAISIN COOKIES

1 cup hot water
1/3 cup shortening
2 cups raisins
2 cups flour
1 tsp. baking powder
1 tsp. baking soda
1 tsp. allspice
1/2 tsp. nutmeg
2 tsp. cinnamon
2 eggs, beaten
1/2 cup applesauce
1 tsp. liquid artificial sweetener
1 tsp. water

Mix hot water, shortening, and raisins. Set aside. Sift flour, baking powder and baking soda. Mix allspice, nutmeg, cinnamon, eggs, applesauce, and sweetener with the 1 tsp. water. Combine flour mixture with egg mixture. Add raisin, water, and shortening mix. Drop by teaspoonfuls onto lightly greased cookie sheet. Bake 8–10 minutes in 350-degree oven. Yields 48 to 50 cookies.

Nutrients per cookie:		Exchanges:	
Calories	53	Bread	1/2
Fat	2g	Fruit	1/4
Cholesterol	11mg	Fat	1/2
Carbohydrate	9g		
Sodium	0mg		

SUGARLESS PEBBLESTONE COOKIES

1 cup raisins
1 (6-oz.) can frozen apple juice concentrate
1/2 cup margarine
1 egg
1 1/4 cups flour
1 tsp. baking soda
1/2 tsp. ground cinnamon
1/2 tsp. finely shredded orange peel
2 cups granola, slightly crushed

In a medium saucepan, heat together raisins, juice concentrate, and margarine until melted. Remove from heat; let cool. Beat in egg. In small mixing bowl combine flour, baking soda, and cinnamon; stir into egg mixture. Stir in orange peel and granola. Let dough stand 1 to 2 minutes or until granola absorbs some of the liquid. Drop by rounded teaspoon 2 inches apart onto ungreased cookie sheets. Bake in 350-degree oven about 10 minutes or until lightly browned on the bottom. Makes about 5–6 dozen.

Note: You can use more spice if desired. Add one of the following: 1/2 tsp. apple-pie mix spice, 1/4 tsp. cloves, 1/4 tsp. ginger, 1/2 tsp. allspice, 1/4 tsp. anise seed (grounded), or 1/4 tsp. nutmeg.

Nutrients per cookie:		Exchanges:	
Calories	54	Bread	1/2
Fat	2g		
Cholesterol	4mg		
Carbohydrate	8g		
Sodium	44mg		

CARROT AND RAISIN COOKIES

2 cups unsifted flour
3/4 cup wheat germ
1 tsp. baking powder
1 tsp. ground cinnamon
1/2 tsp. grated nutmeg
1/2 tsp. ground ginger
Pinch of salt
1 cup oil or shortening
1/4 cup packed brown sugar
2 eggs
1½ cups grated carrot
1 cup raisins

Combine flour, wheat germ, baking powder, spices, salt on wax paper and set aside. Cream oil or shortening and sugar until fluffy. Add eggs and beat. Add carrots and flour mixture to sugar mixture, mixing alternately but beginning and ending with flour. Add raisins. Drop dough from teaspoon on greased baking sheet 1½" apart. Bake at 375 for 10–12 minutes, until lightly browned. Transfer to wire rack to cool. Makes 54 cookies. (Serving is 1 cookie.)

Nutrients per serving:		Exchanges:	
Calories	66	Bread	1/2
Fat	4g	Fat	1/2
Cholesterol	10mg		
Carbohydrate	5g		
Sodium	9mg		

ORANGE CRANBERRY NUT BARS

2 whole eggs
2 egg whites
2/3 cup orange juice
1/4 tsp. orange extract
1/4 cup margarine, softened
2 cups flour
1 tsp. cinnamon
1/2 tsp. baking powder
1 tsp. baking soda
1 cup cranberries, chopped
1/4 tsp. nutmeg
1/3 cup chopped walnuts

In a large bowl beat together the eggs, juice, margarine, orange extract, flour, cinnamon, baking soda and powder until blended. Add cranberries. Spoon into greased and floured 8 x 8 baking dish.

Mix together 1/4 tsp. nutmeg and 1/3 cup chopped walnuts and sprinkle evenly over the top. Bake at 350 for 20 minutes or until an inserted knife comes out clean. Makes 8 servings.

Nutrients per serving:	
Calories	158
Fat	4
Cholesterol	53mg
Carbohydrate	25g
Sodium	53mg

Exchanges:	
Bread	1
Fruit	1
Fat	1

BANANA DATE BARS

Cake:

1 banana (mashed)
1 cup margarine (unsalted, softened)
1 egg
2 egg whites
1 tsp. vanilla
1 1/4 cups water
3 cups flour
1 tsp. baking soda
2 tsp. baking powder
3/4 cup chopped dates

Topping:

1/3 cup chopped dates
1/3 cup English walnuts, chopped
1/3 cup flaked coconut

Beat mashed banana and margarine until creamy. Add eggs, vanilla, and water. Beat. Add flour, baking soda, baking powder and beat well. Stir in 3/4 cup dates. Spoon batter into an oiled and floured 9 x 13-inch baking pan. Spread batter evenly in pan.

Combine topping ingredients and sprinkle over batter. Bake at 350 degrees for 20 to 25 minutes, or until a knife inserted in the center comes out clean. Cool on wire rack. Makes 30 squares.

Nutrients per serving:		Exchanges:	
Calories	133	Bread	1/2
Fat	7g	Fruit	1/2
Cholesterol	9mg	Fat	1
Carbohydrate	15g		
Sodium	40mg		

LIGHT COCONUT BARS

1/4 cup regular margarine
1/2 cup Raisin Bran
1/4 cup brown sugar
1 tsp. Sweet 'N Low brown sugar
1 egg
1 tsp. vanilla
3/4 cup flour
1/2 tsp. baking powder
1/8 tsp. baking soda
1/3 cup shredded coconut
Vegetable spray

Melt the margarine, then add cereal and cook for 2 minutes. Stir constantly to prevent sticking. Remove from heat and mix in the Sweet 'N Low brown sugar, egg, and vanilla. Set aside.

Add the rest of the ingredients and mix well. Spray an 8-inch square pan with the vegetable spray and spread the mixture evenly. Bake at 350 for 18 minutes. Cover and store in the refrigerator. Yields 16 bars.

Nutrients per serving:		Exchanges:	
Calories	90	Bread	1
Fat	4g	Fat	1
Cholesterol	13.3mg		
Carbohydrate	12g		
Sodium	76mg		

ICE CREAM

Vanilla:

1 egg
1 egg white
1/4 cup sugar (192 calories)
1 cup sugar substitute (Equal)
1/8 tsp. salt
1 qt. skim milk

Mix well. Pour into ice cream freezer. Add milk to fill to within 2 inches of top. Freeze.
Variations: Add 2 bananas, finely diced. Or add 1 cup peaches or strawberries, puréed and mixed with the 1/4 cup of sugar. Mix and allow to chill for 1 hour before making ice cream. Calories — About 66 per 1/2 cup.

Note: This recipe is adapted from Warrings' Ice Cream Paulor. It makes a half gallon.

Nutrients per serving:					Exchanges:	
	Vanilla	*Banana*	*Peach*	*Straw.*		
Calories	66	80	71	69	Milk	1/2
Fat	1g	1g	1g	1g	Fruit	1/2
Cholesterol	22mg	22mg	22mg	22mg	(except vanilla)	
Carbohydrate	9g	10g	9g	9g		
Sodium	69mg	69mg	69mg	69mg		

CHERRY SAUCE

2 cups chopped frozen cherries
$1\frac{1}{2}$ tsp. cornstarch
2–3 pkgs. Equal
1 tsp. lemon juice

Mix cherries and cornstarch. Cook until boiling and thick. Remove from heat. Cool 2 minutes, then add Equal and lemon juice. Mix well. Use to top desserts. Serves 4.

Nutrients per serving:		Exchanges:	
Calories	19	Fruit	1/3
Fat	0		
Cholesterol	0		
Carbohydrate	4g		
Sodium	3mg		

BLUEBERRY SAUCE

2 cups frozen, unsweetened blueberries
1/2 tsp. cornstarch
1 Tbs. lemon juice
2 or 3 pkg. Equal

Cook blueberries, lemon juice, and cornstarch until boiling and thick. Remove from heat. Cool 2 minutes, then add Equal. Mix well. Use to top desserts. Serves 4.

Nutrients per serving:		Exchanges:	
Calories	17	Fruit	1/3
Fat	0		
Cholesterol	0		
Carbohydrate	4g		
Sodium	3mg		

SUGARLESS CRANBERRY SAUCE

1/2 cup water
2 Tbs. grated orange rind
Liquid Sweet'N Low (to equal 1 c. sugar)
1/4 tsp. salt
1/8 tsp. cinnamon
1 dash of cloves, optional
4 cups fresh ripe cranberries
12 tsp. vanilla

Combine water, orange rind, sugar substitute, salt, cinnamon, and cloves in saucepan. Bring to boil; simmer 5 minutes, stirring occasionally. Add cranberries; simmer until skin pops.

Remove from heat and add vanilla. Refrigerate until serving time. Yields 3 3/4 cups. (2 Tbs. per serving).

Nutrients per serving:		Exchanges:	
Calories	28	Fruit	1
Fat	0		
Cholesterol	0		
Carbohydrates	12		
Sodium	10		

MOM'S GUMDROP CANDY

1 can fruit-flavored diet drink
1/2 cup lemon juice
1/2 tsp. vanilla
5 envelopes unflavored gelatin

Heat half the diet drink to boiling. Mix the rest of the ingredients with the remaining half of diet drink. Put in an 8 x 8-inch (or 7 x 7-inch) baking dish. Slowly pour in boiling drink and stir until gelatin is dissolved. Put in refrigerator until firm. Cut into shapes; use cookie cutter if desired.

Nutrients per serving:		Exchanges:
Calories	8	This is a freebie.
Fat	0	
Cholesterol	0	
Carbohydrate	.6g	
Sodium	0	

Note: For fruit flavor, use $1\frac{1}{2}$ cups fruit juice instead of diet drink.

Nutrients per serving:		Exchanges:	
Calories	25	Fruit	1/3
Fat	0		
Cholesterol	0		
Carbohydrate	5g		
Sodium	0		

FOUR SQUARE CANDY

4 envelopes unflavored gelatin
4 pkg. flavored gelatin (3 oz. each) (sugar-free)
4 cups boiling water

Add together in large bowl and stir until gelatin dissolves. Pour into shallow sheet pan and chill until firm. Use cookie cutter or knife to cut shapes, then carefully remove with a spatula.

Note: Leftover chopped gelatin can be put into apple salad or whipped cream.

Nutrients per serving:		Exchanges:
Calories	96 in whole batch	None

For a third less calories, eat ice milk instead of ice cream.

Meats, Fish, and Main Dishes

Pull off Chicken Skin to Save Fat, Calories and Cholesterol

3 1/2 oz. cooked chicken	Grams fat	Calories
Light meat with skin	10.9	222
Light meat without skin	4.5	173
Dark meat with skin	15.8	253
Dark meat without skin	9.7	205

Source: U.S. Department of Health and Human Services

High-fat Meats Have More Than Twice as Much Fat as Lean Meats

1 oz. meat	Grams fat	Grams protein	Calories
Lean (beef round, veal chops, skinned chicken, boiled ham)	3	7	55
Medium (pork chops, pot roast, ground beef, steak)	5	7	75
High (prime rib, spareribs)	8	7	100

Source: *Exchange Lists for Meal Planning*, by the American Diabetes Association, Inc., and the American Dietetic Association

TERRY'S CHICKEN

- 1 (7-oz.) pkg. Macaroni Creamettes or elbow macaroni
- 2 cans (5 oz.) chicken
- 1 can Campbell's chicken broth
- 1 can Campbell's Healthy Request Cream of Mushroom Soup (less salt)
- 1/2 cup grated sharp cheddar cheese (2 oz.)

Put in greased 9 x 13-inch pan. Chill overnight, or freeze for later use. Next day bake at 350 degrees for 1 hour. Serves 6.

Will keep in freezer for up to 3 months.

Note: Heart patients, this dish has almost the full ration of sodium for a main dish, so don't eat anything else high in sodium at the same meal. (Each meat exchange includes 4–6 grams fat.)

Nutrients per serving:		Exchanges:	
Calories	285	Bread	2
Fat	10g	Meat	2
Cholesterol	14mg	Fat	1/2
Carbohydrate	30g		
Sodium	779mg		

CHICKEN WITH WILD RICE

1 pkg. (6-oz.) wild rice
1/4 cup margarine
1/3 cup chopped onion
1/3 cup flour
1 tsp. No Salt salt
1 cup water
1 cup chicken broth
2 cups cooked chicken, cubed
1/3 cup diced pimiento
1/3 cup chopped fresh parsley
1/4 cup slivered almonds

Cook rice with seasoning packet according to pkg. directions. Melt margarine while rice is cooking. Add onion to margarine and cook until tender; stir in flour and No Salt. Slowly add water and the chicken broth. Cook, stirring constantly until thickened. Stir in chicken, pimiento, parsley, almonds, and cooked rice. Pour into a 2-qt. greased casserole dish. Bake at 400 degrees, uncovered, for 30 minutes. Serves 8.

Note: You can use 1/2 wild rice and 1/2 brown rice or white rice.

Nutrients per serving:		Exchanges:	
Calories	157	Bread	1
Fat	6g	Meat	1
Cholesterol	30mg	Fat	1/2
Carbohydrate	12g		
Sodium	180mg		

To make your own poultry spice use: 1/2 tsp. each of sage, marjoram, allspice, rosemary, and thyme. Mash together on a small plate with a spoon. Store in a closed container.

SAUCY CHICKEN AND BROCCOLI

- 8 pieces of chicken (legs, thighs, breasts)
- 2 cans Campbell's Low Sodium Cream of Mushroom Soup
- 1/2 cup skim milk
- 5 pieces of Borden's Lite Line Sharp Cheddar Cheese, grated
- 1/2 cup Miracle Whip Light
- 1/4 cup slivered almonds
- 1/4 cup grated Parmesan cheese
- Large head of broccoli, cooked
- 1½ cups raw rice (simmer in 3 cups boiling water 15 minutes)

Boil the chicken for 8 minutes. Remove skin. (For company dish, use only chicken breasts and remove the bones.) Place in an 8 x 11-inch baking dish. Scald the soup and milk. Add grated cheese and Miracle Whip. Stir with wire whisk until well blended. Pour sauce over chicken and bake at 350 degrees for 25 minutes. Sprinkle Parmesan cheese over top and bake 5 minutes more. Serves 8 with plenty of sauce to pour over rice and broccoli. (1 serving = 1 piece of meat and 1/2 cup each rice and broccoli.)

Nutrients per serving:		Exchanges:	
Calories	279	Bread	1/2
Fat	14g	Meat	2
Cholesterol	69mg	Fat	1
Carbohydrate	7g		
Sodium	400mg		

BREADED BAKED CHICKEN

- 1/4 cup unseasoned dry breadcrumbs
- 1/4 tsp. garlic powder
- 1/4 tsp. paprika
- 1 Tbs. grated Parmesan cheese
- 4 pieces of chicken (coating is enough for 6 pieces)

Remove skin from chicken. Roll in mixture of crumbs, garlic powder, paprika, and Parmesan cheese. Bake uncovered for 50–60 minutes at 350. For microwave, cook on high (full power) for 10 minutes; rotate dish and cook 7–10 minutes more. Warning: Check near the end of time. Meat can dry out quickly if overdone.

Nutrients per piece of chicken:		Exchanges:	
Calories (108 breast, 173 thigh)		Bread	1/3
Fat	3.3g	Meat	1
Cholesterol	58mg		
Carbohydrate	4.5g		
Sodium	110mg		

The Department of Health and Human Services recommends you eat less red meat and more chicken.

TOMATO CHICKEN AND RICE

- 3 large chicken legs (thighs included), cut into 6 pieces
- 1 cup long grain rice, raw
- 3/4 tsp. salt substitute
- 2 cups water
- 1/2 tsp. garlic powder
- 1 tsp. Worcestershire sauce (suggest Lea and Perrin)
- 1/4 cup catsup (suggest Del Monte)
- 8 oz. can tomato sauce (low sodium)
- 1½ Tbs. dry minced onion
- 1/4 cup water

Place rice, salt substitute, and 2 cups water in a baking dish (large 8-inch-square Corningware dish). Nestle chicken pieces on top. Mix other ingredients in bowl and spoon over chicken. Bake for one hour in oven preheated to 350 F. (If you use microwave, it will take almost as long.) Serves 6.

Nutrients per serving:		Exchanges:	
Calories	192	Bread	1½
Fat	0	Meat	1
Cholesterol	20mg	Vegetables	1½
Carbohydrate	31g		
Sodium	388mg		

CHICKEN AND SPUDS

- 4 small to medium potatoes
- 2 meaty leg quarters
- 1 can Campbell's Cream of Mushroom Soup (1/3 less salt)

Set oven at 350 degrees. Peel potatoes. Cut up and place in bottom of 8-inch-square Corningware casserole. Skin chicken and cut quarters into legs and thighs. Place on top of potatoes. Spread undiluted cream of mushroom soup on top of chicken. Bake 1 hour, uncovered. Serves 4.

Nutrients per serving:		Exchanges:	
Calories	78	Bread	2
Fat	6g	Meat	1
Cholesterol	5mg	Milk	1/2
Carbohydrate	36g		
Sodium	388mg		

1/2 cup chopped or diced white chicken meat equals one chicken breast.

PLUM GOOD CHICKEN

6 pieces chicken (legs and thighs)
2 Tbs. margarine
3 Tbs. cornstarch
1/4 tsp. salt substitute
1/4 tsp. ginger
1/4 cup cold water
1 tsp. no salt added bouillon crystals
2/3 cup boiling water
1/2 cup orange juice
3 Tbs. plum jelly (can use grape jelly)
1 orange, unpeeled, sliced, quartered

Brown chicken in margarine; place in baking pan. Mix cornstarch, salt, and ginger with 1/4 cup cold water. Dissolve bouillon in 2/3 cup boiling water. Mix that with orange juice and jelly. Heat until jelly melts. Then stir in cornstarch mixture. Cook sauce, stirring constantly, until it thickens and becomes clear. Pour sauce over chicken. Top with orange slices. Bake at 350 for 1 hour or until tender. Baste occasionally. Serves 6.

Nutrients per serving:		Exchanges:	
Calories	108	Bread	1/2
Fat	4.3g	Meat	1
Cholesterol	10mg	Fruit	1/2
Carbohydrate	15g		
Sodium	94mg		

CHICKEN WITH LEMON GRAVY

6 chicken breasts or thighs
1 Tbs. cornstarch
1 cup evaporated skim milk
1 cup boiling water
1/4 tsp. No Salt salt
1 Borden's low sodium chicken bouillon cube
2 Tbs. lemon juice
1/2 tsp. cardamom
2 Tbs. grated Parmesan cheese

Skin chicken and brown lightly on both sides in a Teflon skillet. Remove meat and place in baking dish. Mix cornstarch with a little of the milk and stir until lumps are dissolved. Add boiling water, No Salt, bouillon, lemon juice, and cardamom. Cook, stirring constantly, in skillet until slightly thickened. Pour sauce over chicken and sprinkle top with Parmesan cheese. Place under heated broiler until delicately browned in spots. Serves 6.

Nutrients per serving:		Exchanges:	
Calories	187	Meat	1 1/2
Fat	4g	Milk	1/2
Cholesterol	75mg		
Carbohydrate	5g		
Sodium	299mg		

One tablespoon cornstarch thickens sauces as well as 2 Tbs. flour and has half the calories.

CHICKEN 'N SPICE

6 pieces chicken, cut up
1 tsp. No Salt salt
2 Tbs. lemon juice
1/2 tsp. allspice
1 Tbs. brown SugarTwin
(Pepper if desired)

Place chicken on broiler pan, skin side up (for less fat, remove skin, but be sure to moisten well with lemon juice). Broil chicken until golden. Brush chicken with lemon juice or rub with cut piece of lemon. Sprinkle with mixture of salt, allspice, and brown sugar. Return to broiler until brown on top, then turn and brush with lemon juice and sprinkle with spice mixture (15 minutes per side is the usual time required for a total of 30 minutes cooking time). Serves 4.

Nutrients per serving:		Exchanges:	
Calories	217	Meat	3
Fat	4g		
Cholesterol	109mg		
Carbohydrate	0		
Sodium	96mg		

QUICK HERBED CHICKEN

6 pieces chicken, skinned (legs, thighs, 1/2 breasts)
1 cup catsup (Hunt's Low Sodium)
1 tsp. poultry seasoning (measure herbs and spices onto saucer and mash together with spoon: 1/2 tsp. each sage, marjoram, allspice, rosemary and thyme)

Mix catsup with poultry seasoning. Dip chicken pieces in mixture and place in uncovered Corningware casserole. Microwave on high for 10 minutes. Rotate casserole and microwave on high for another 7–10 minutes. Serves 4.

Note: Bake in regular oven at 350 for 30 to 40 minutes.

Nutrients per serving:	1/2 Breast	Leg	Thigh	Exchanges:	
Calories	188	106	138	Meat	2–2½
Fat	3g	2g	2.5g	Vegetable	2
Chol.	73mg	41mg	50mg		
Carb.	11.5g	11.5g	11.5g		
Sod.	64mg	42mg	50mg		

Darker fish and the dark meat of poultry are much higher in fat than the lighter meat.

MIKE-BAKED CHICKEN

1 tsp. salt substitute
1/2 tsp. pepper
1/4 tsp. allspice
4 Tbs. water
1/2 cup catsup (Hunt's no salt added)
10 tsp. Sweet 'n Low brown sugar
3 leg quarters (skinned and cut into 6 pieces)

Mix first 6 ingredients. Dip chicken pieces into mixture. Microwave on high for 10 minutes. Rotate casserole and microwave on high for 7–10 minutes more. Serves 4.

Nutrients per serving:		Exchanges:	
Calories	112	Bread	1
Fat	1g	Meat	1
Cholesterol	30mg	Vegetable	1
Carbohydrate	19g		
Sodium	47mg		

MICROWAVE CHICKEN MARJORAM

3 lbs. cut-up chicken
3/4 cup catsup (recommend Del Monte low sodium)
6 Tbs. water
1 1/2 cups dry breadcrumbs
1 1/2 tsp. marjoram
3/4 tsp. basil
1 1/2 tsp. oregano
1 1/2 tsp. garlic powder
3 tsp. paprika

Remove skin from chicken. Mix catsup and water. Mix crumbs and spices. Dip chicken in catsup mixture, then roll in crumbs. Place in microwave-safe baking dish so that pieces do not overlap. Microwave for 10 minutes on high or full power, then rotate dish (180 degrees) and microwave for 10 more minutes. Meaty pieces may take a little longer to cook. Serves 8.

Nutrients per serving:		Exchanges:	
Calories	310	Bread	1
Fat	1g	Meat	3
Cholesterol	28mg	Vegetables	1
Carbohydrate	19g		
Sodium	287mg		

CHICKEN ITALIAN

3 lbs. chicken pieces
1/3 cup Kraft Zesty Italian Reduced Calorie Dressing
1/2 cup breadcrumbs
1 tsp. oregano
1/8 tsp. garlic powder
1/4 cup grated Romano or Parmesan cheese

Skin and marinate chicken in dressing for 20 minutes. Mix crumbs, seasoning, and cheese. Roll chicken in mixture. Place in microwave baking dish. Do not crowd pieces. Microwave 10 minutes on high. Turn dish 180 degrees. Microwave 10 or more minutes on high. The meaty pieces may take longer. Serves 8.

Nutrients per serving:		Exchanges:	
Calories	271	Bread	1/3
Fat	4g	Meat	3
Cholesterol	33mg		
Carbohydrate	6g		
Sodium	304mg		

CHICKEN 'N PEPPERS

6 pieces chicken, skinned
1/2 cup onions, chopped
1 8-oz. can Hunt's No Salt Added Tomato Sauce
1 20-oz. can Hunt's No Salt Added Tomato Sauce
2 cups fresh mushrooms, sliced
1 cup fresh green pepper, chopped
2 Tbs. oil

Lightly brown both sides of chicken in oil. Remove and place in a casserole dish. Sauté mushrooms and green pepper in same oil. Add tomato sauce to mushrooms and peppers. Pour over chicken. Microwave on high for about 10 minutes. Rotate 1/2 turn and cook another 8 minutes more. Serves 6.

Note: Serve on a bed of rice.

Nutrients per serving:		Exchanges:	
Calories	208	Meat	2
Fat	7g	Vegetable	2½
Cholesterol	57mg		
Carbohydrate	13g		
Sodium	168mg		

Every gram of fat squeezed from a dish saves 9 calories.

PIQUANT BAKED CHICKEN

3 skinless legs and thighs, cut up
1/2 cup plain lowfat yogurt
1/2 tsp. garlic powder
2 tsp. flour
1/4 tsp. allspice
1/4 tsp. cardamom
1/4 tsp. ginger
1 Tbs. lemon juice

Place chicken in 8 x 8 inch Corningware casserole. Mix rest of ingredients and spread over chicken. Set microwave oven on warm or defrost setting and cook 10 minutes. Baste chicken with juices in pan and cook 15–20 minutes on high. Rotate 1/2 turn at least once during cooking. Serves 4.

Nutrients per serving:	
Calories	183
Fat	1g
Cholesterol	113mg
Carbohydrates	4g
Sodium	143mg

Exchanges:	
Meat	1 1/2
Milk	1/3

CHICKEN MICHAEL

3 pieces of skinned chicken (legs, thighs)
1/2 tsp. oregano
1/2 tsp. basil
1 tsp. Worcestershire sauce (Lea and Perrin's)
3/4 cup catsup (Del Monte)
1/2 tsp. cinnamon
1/8 tsp. garlic powder

Put chicken pieces in sealable sandwich bag. Mix rest of ingredients and pour in bag. Seal bag and place in bowl because bag may break. Microwave on high 10 minutes or until done. Rotate bowl once during cooking unless you use a turntable so the heat will be distributed evenly. Serves 3.

Nutrients per serving:	
Calories	152
Fat	2g
Cholesterol	14mg
Carbohydrate	17g
Sodium	243mg

Exchanges:	
Bread	1
Meat	2

(*Note:* Although there is no bread in this recipe, the catsup has 17 grams of carbohydrate, but a vegetable exchange only allows 5 grams of carbohydrate. Therefore this is counted as a bread exchange.)

ORIENTAL CHICKEN ON POTATO

3 skinless chicken breast halves or 3 pieces (2 thighs and 1 leg) cut in bite-size pieces
2 large carrots, quarter lengthwise, cut in 2 inch pieces
1½ cups frozen green beans
1 medium onion, sliced
2 tsp. vegetable oil
1 tsp. ground ginger
1 Tbs. cornstarch
1/2 cup chicken broth (boil bones with water)
2 tsp. light soy sauce
4 medium potatoes

Combine chicken, green beans, carrots, onion, vegetable oil and ginger in 2-qt. casserole dish. Cover dish with plastic wrap and microwave on high 5 minutes. Stir, rotate the dish, and cook 3 minutes more or until chicken turns white.

Mix the cornstarch, broth, and soy sauce in a small bowl. Add to chicken and stir well. Cook on high for 5 minutes more. Bake potatoes for 6–8 minutes. If necessary, reheat chicken. Cut lengthwise slit in each potato and fluff it open. Pour chicken mixture over it. Serves 4.

Note: You may substitute 1/4 lb. snow peas or 1 cup green pepper strips for green beans or use 1/3 cup cooked rice instead of potato with little change in nutrients or exchanges.

Nutrients per serving:		Exchanges:	
Calories	329	Bread	2
Fat	13g	Meat	3
Cholesterol	38mg	Vegetable	2
Carbohydrate	38g		
Sodium	165mg		

CHICKEN ROSEMARY

- 2 chicken leg quarters, skinned
- 1 Tbs. vegetable oil
- 1 medium onion, chopped
- 1 tsp. sugar
- 1 chicken bouillon cube (low-sodium)
- 1 cup boiling water
- 2 Tbs. lemon juice
- 1/2 tsp. rubbed thyme
- 2 tsp. rosemary
- 1/8 tsp. garlic powder
- 1/4 tsp. black pepper

Separate legs from thighs. Brown chopped onion in oil in nonstick frying pan; add 1 tsp. sugar and cook for a minute. Add other ingredients and mix well. Place chicken pieces in casserole dish and pour mixture over. Cover and microwave on high for 10 minutes. Spoon liquid over chicken and rotate dish for even cooking. Remove cover and cook 10 minutes more. Serves 4.

Nutrients per serving:	
Calories	241
Fat	10g
Cholesterol	50mg
Carbohydrate	5g
Sodium	50mg

Exchanges:	
Meat	2
Vegetable	1
Fat	1/2

SWISSED CHICKEN

- 8 pieces skinless chicken, removed from bone (2 thighs and 2 legs, or 4½ breasts)
- 1 Tbs. margarine
- 1/2 green pepper
- 4 oz. fresh mushrooms
- 1 lg. onion, sliced
- 1/4 tsp. garlic powder
- 2 cups Hunt's Tomato Juice (low-sodium)

Brown chicken pieces in melted margarine and remove from pan. Cook onions, peppers, and mushrooms until onions are almost transparent. (Add mushrooms toward the last. They don't need much cooking.) Add chicken, garlic powder, and tomato juice. Simmer for twenty minutes. Yields 8 (1/2 cup) servings. Serve over 1/3 cup of rice.

Nutrients per serving:		With Rice
Calories	81.5	194
Fat	3g	3g
Cholesterol	9mg	0
Carbohydrate	8g	28g
Sodium	420mg	420mg

Exchanges:		With Rice
Bread	1/2	2
Meat	1	1

CRISPY BAKED CHICKEN

3 lbs. chicken parts, skinned
1/2 cup evaporated skim milk
1 cup cornflake crumbs
1/2 tsp. salt
1/4 tsp. pepper

Mix salt, pepper and crumbs. Dip chicken in milk, then roll in crumb mixture. Place in shallow pan lined with aluminum foil. Do not crowd pieces. Bake at 350 for 1 hour. (1 serving is 1 thigh or 1 breast, or 2 legs, or a leg and 2 wings.)

Note: You will probably have some milk and crumbs left over. For 3 legs and 1 thigh, it takes less than half a cup.

Nutrients per serving:	
Calories	235
Fat	5g
Cholesterol	77mg
Carbohydrate	13g
Sodium	330mg

Exchanges:	
Bread	1
Meat	3½

ALOHA CHICKEN

2½ lbs. chicken pieces, skinned
2 Borden Low Sodium Chicken Bouillon Cubes
1 Tbs. margarine
1 cup diced green pepper (1 med. pepper)
1 cup thinly sliced radishes
1 cup canned pineapple chunks (unsweetened)
1/2 cup juice from pineapple
1 tsp. light soy sauce
2 Tbs. flour
Dash pepper
4½ cups cooked rice
Chow mein noodles (if desired)

Simmer the chicken in water with bouillon cubes. Remove meat from bones and cut into chunks. Save 1 cup of chicken broth. While chicken is cooking, melt margarine in frying pan or wok and sauté the radishes, green peppers, and pineapple until crisp tender, but not brown. (Put rice on to cook.) Mix 1 cup saved chicken broth with 1/2 cup pineapple juice and 1 tsp. soy sauce. Add to pan.

Mix flour with 1 Tbs. cold water and stir to remove lumps. Add to vegetables. Add cut up chicken and a dash of pepper, and cook until everything is hot. Serve over rice. If desired, sprinkle chow mein noodles on top. Serves 6.

(Portion is 3/4 cup mixture served over 3/4 cup cooked rice.)

Nutrients per serving:		Exchanges:	
Calories	310	Bread	$2^1/_2$
Fat	7g	Meat	2
Cholesterol	58mg		
Carbohydrate	39g		
Sodium	314mg		

THYME CHICKEN

$1^1/_4$ lbs. chicken, skinned (or 3 Cornish hens halved)
1/2 tsp. salt
1/8 tsp. pepper
Thyme to taste (1/8–1 tsp.)

Place in slow-cooker. Sprinkle seasonings on top and cook on low for 4 hours. Serve in 3-oz. helpings (6 servings). Serve with tossed salad and wild rice.

Nutrients per serving:		Exchanges:	
Calories	150	Meat	2
Fat	4g		
Cholesterol	82mg		
Carbohydrate	0g		
Sodium	231mg		

CHICKEN SPAGHETTI

- 3 large chicken leg-quarters, skinned
- 8 oz. raw spaghetti
- 4 large mushrooms, sliced, or 4 oz. canned (drained)
- 1 large onion, thinly sliced
- 1 Tbs. margarine
- 2 (15-oz.) cans Hunt's No Salt Added Tomato Sauce
- 6 pieces of Lite-Line Sharp Cheddar Process Cheese, grated

Skin chicken and boil in water until tender. Cook spaghetti in large pan of boiling water until tender.

While chicken and spaghetti are cooking, sauté onion and mushrooms in margarine until onion is limp and mushrooms start to brown. Cut up cooked chicken; drain spaghetti. Add both to vegetables and mix in tomato sauce. Cook until all are hot and sauce has thickened a little (about 5–10 minutes). Serve hot with grated cheese sprinkled on top. Yields 5 (1-cup) servings.

Nutrients per serving:		Exchanges:	
Calories	262	Bread	1 1/2
Fat	6g	Meat	1 1/2
Cholesterol	60mg	Vegetable	1
Carbohydrate	28g		
Sodium	129mg		

BAKED RICE AND CHICKEN

- 2 chicken leg quarters, skinned and cut into pieces
- 1/8 tsp. garlic powder
- 1/2 tsp. Molly McButter
- 1/4 tsp. marjoram
- 1 cup raw rice
- 3 cups water
- 3 chicken bouillon cubes (very low sodium)

Mix all but chicken in 2-quart Corningware casserole. Lay chicken on top. Bake 1 hour at 350. Stir after 30 minutes. Serves 4. Figured on the basis of 6 servings rice.

Nutrients per serving:		Exchanges:	
Calories	373	Bread	2 1/2
Fat	10.6g	Meat	3
Cholesterol	50mg		
Carbohydrate	38g		
Sodium	39mg		

TURKEY OR CHICKEN TETRAZZINI

8 oz. raw spaghetti noodles (cook in water and drain)
1 can Campbell's Healthy Request Mushroom Soup (low salt)
1/2 cup skim milk
3 cups diced turkey or chicken
1 (4-oz.) can mushroom pieces or 6 large fresh ones
1 Tbs. parsley flakes
4 slices lowfat sharp processed cheddar cheese, grated
1 tsp. No Salt salt
1/4 tsp. pepper (optional)

Combine in 2-qt. casserole. Bake at 400 degrees 15 minutes or until heated through. Serves 6.

Nutrients per serving:		Exchanges:	
Calories	222	Bread	1
Fat	7g	Meat	1
Cholesterol	57mg	Vegetable	1
Carbohydrate	15g		
Sodium	332mg		

CHILI CHEESE BAKE

1 lb. ground beef, browned, drained
1 lb. pkg. spaghetti, cooked
1 (15-oz.) can tomatoes
1 (15-oz.) can red beans
1/2 tsp. melted margarine
2 Tbs. dried onion
Salt, pepper, chili powder (about 1/4 tsp. each to taste)
1/2 cup shredded sharp cheddar cheese for topping

Add all ingredients together in a 2-qt. covered casserole dish. Bake at 350 degrees for 20 minutes, then remove to sprinkle shredded cheese over top. Return to oven for 5–7 minutes until cheese is melted. Serves 6.

Nutrients per serving:		Exchanges:	
Calories	303	Bread	1½
Fat	6g	Meat	2
Cholesterol	52mg	Vegetable	1
Carbohydrate	25g		
Sodium	413mg		

MEXICAN GOOLASH

- 1/2 lb. lean ground beef
- 1/2 cup chopped onions
- 1/4 cup chopped green peppers
- 3 cups tomato juice (Hunt's No Salt Added)
- 1½ cups raw macaroni
- 1/4 tsp. garlic powder
- 1/4 tsp. pepper
- 1/4 tsp. chili powder

Add macaroni to boiling water and cook for 7 minutes. Cook the first 3 ingredients in cast-iron skillet until meat is brown and vegetables are tender. Drain off fat. Add tomato juice, macaroni, and spices. Simmer until liquid is almost absorbed. Serves 4.

Note: Served with a salad, this makes a delicious meal.

Nutrients per serving:		Exchanges:	
Calories	323	Bread	2
Fat	11g	Meat	2
Cholesterol	49mg	Vegetable	1
Carbohydrate	36g		
Sodium	64mg		

BEEF JARDINIERE

- 1/2 cup fresh or frozen green beans
- 6 small carrots, sliced (about 1½ cups)
- 1/2 tsp. salt substitute
- 1/2 lb. lean ground beef
- 1 medium onion, chopped
- 1/2 cup frozen corn
- 8 oz. tomato sauce, no salt added
- 1/4 tsp. garlic powder

Cook the green beans and carrots in boiling water with salt substitute. Brown the ground beef with the chopped onions. Place 2 paper towels in a colander and drain the ground beef and onions. Return to frying pan and add the carrots and green beans. Cook until vegetables are almost tender and the cooking liquid is almost evaporated.

Add corn, tomato sauce, and garlic powder. Put in 8-inch round or square baking dish. Bake in preheated 350-degree oven for about 10 minutes or until heated through and not runny. For microwave, cook on high for 5 minutes. Serves 4.

Nutrients per serving:		Exchanges:	
Calories	178	Bread	1
Fat	8g	Meat	2
Cholesterol	37mg	Vegetable	1
Carbohydrate	18g		
Sodium	62mg		

RICE-A-PIE

- 2/3 cup raw rice (need 2 cups cooked)
- 3/4 tsp. salt substitute
- 1 tsp. dry onion (or 1 Tbs. chopped fresh)
- 2 cups water
- 3/4 cup carrots, thinly sliced
- 3/4 cup frozen peas
- 3/4 cup frozen corn
- 2 Tbs. dry onion (soak in 1/4 cup water) or 1/4 cup chopped
- 1/2 lb. lean ground beef
- 1 cup catsup, low-sodium type
- 1 Tbs. margarine, melted
- 1/4 tsp. marjoram
- 1 beaten egg
- 1 slice sharp cheddar process cheese (use Borden's Lite Line)

Put rice, 1/4 tsp. salt substitute, and 1 tsp. dry onion in boiling water. Cover and cook over low heat 15 minutes or until rice is done and water is absorbed. Cook carrots until almost tender. Drain carrots. Add carrots, frozen corn, and frozen peas to the rice and turn off heat.

Brown onion and ground beef. Drain in a colander. Return to pan and mix in 1/2 tsp. salt substitute, catsup, and 1/4 cup water. Add the margarine, marjoram, and beaten egg to the rice. Mix and press into bottom and sides of 9-inch pie pan. Fill with meat mixture, and top with grated cheese. Bake at 350 for 20 minutes. Serves 6.

Nutrients per serving:		Exchanges:	
Calories	306	Bread	2
Fat	10g	Meat (includes fat)	2
Cholesterol	77mg	Vegetable	1
Carbohydrate	40g		
Sodium	99mg		

HUNTER STEW

1 lb. pkg. egg noodles
1 lb. lean ground beef
1 medium onion, diced
1 can low-sodium cream of mushroom soup
1 can creamed corn
Seasoning to taste

Cook and drain noodles. Brown meat and onion together. Drain off excess grease and add noodles. Mix cream of mushroom soup and creamed corn to noodles. Season. Let simmer for about 30 minutes. May add a little water if so desired. Serves 8.

Nutrients per serving:		Exchanges:	
Calories	231	Bread	1
Fat	10g	Fat	1
Cholesterol	37mg	Meat	1
Carbohydrate	20g	Vegetable	1
Sodium	98mg		

Pay special attention to the sodium and cholesterol on labels.

SPAGHETTI JARDINIERE

4 oz. fine noodles (not egg)
1/2 lb. lean ground beef
1 medium onion, chopped
1 cup frozen green peas
1 cup frozen corn
1 (15-oz.) can tomato sauce, salt-free
2 tsp. Worcestershire sauce
1/4 tsp. garlic powder
4 slices lowfat American cheese

Cook noodles in boiling water for the minimum time recommended on the package (generally 6–8 minutes).

Brown ground beef and chopped onion in nonstick frying pan until meat is browned and onions start to become transparent. Pour into a colander and let drain well. (To eliminate even more fat, you can rinse briefly with hot water.)

Return meat and onions to frying pan and add all other ingredients except cheese. Mix and cook about 5 minutes or until vegetables are done. Grate half a slice of cheese over each serving. Serves 8.

Nutrients per serving:		Exchanges:	
Calories	125	Bread	1/2
Fat	4g	Meat	1
Cholesterol	19mg	Vegetable	1/2
Carbohydrate	10g		
Sodium	55mg		

CORKSCREW CASSEROLE

1½ cups vegetable corkscrew noodles (green, orange, white)
1/2 lb. lean ground beef
1 large onion, choppped
1/2 cup frozen green beans
2 medium carrots, sliced
1/2 cup frozen peas
1 can low-sodium cream of mushroom soup
1 cup skim milk
1/4 tsp. marjoram

Cook noodles in plenty of boiling water for 5 minutes. Brown ground beef with onions and drain in a colander to remove grease. Pour cooked noodles and water on top of meat to drain.

Cook green beans and carrots in a small amount of water in a 2-qt. casserole dish in the microwave until crisp tender (about 6 minutes on high; or cook in boiling water on stove). Drain beans and carrots, and mix all the ingredients in a 2-qt. casserole dish. Microwave on high until peas are done and everything is hot — about 5 minutes on high (or about 10 minutes in oven at 350). Makes 5 (1-cup) servings.

Nutrients per serving:		Exchanges:	
Calories	362	Bread	2
Fat	14g	Meat	1
Cholesterol	42mg	Vegetable	1
Carbohydrate	33g	Fat	2
Sodium	219mg		

LASAGNA

1/2 lb. lean ground beef
1 large onion, chopped
1 tsp. oregano
1 tsp. basil
1/4 tsp. garlic powder
1 (15-oz.) can Hunt's Tomato Sauce (no salt added type)
3/4 cup catsup (Del Monte low-sodium type)
1/4 cup water
9 lasagna noodles (cook 8 minutes in boiling water)
12 oz. lowfat cottage cheese
6 fresh mushrooms, sliced about 3/4 cup
2 Tbs. Parmesan cheese

Brown ground beef with chopped onions. Mix oregano, basil, garlic powder, tomato sauce, catsup, and water with browned ground beef and onions. Spread a little sauce on bottom of 8 x 11-inch pan. Lay 3 lasagna noodles in pan. Spread one-third of the cottage cheese and one-third of the mushrooms over that. Spread one-third of the sauce that's left on top. Repeat with 2 more layers of lasagna, cottage cheese, mushrooms, and sauce.

Sprinkle Parmesan cheese on top and cook in microwave on high for 10 minutes (15–20 minutes at 350 in regular oven) or until hot. If you bake in the oven, you may need to use more sauce (add 3 Tbs. catsup, 1 Tbs. water) to keep it from drying out. Serves 6.

Nutrients per serving:		Exchanges:	
Calories	397	Bread	3
Fat	10g	Meat	3
Cholesterol	37mg	Vegetable	2
Carbohydrate	54g		
Sodium	271mg		

SPINACH LASAGNA

Make the same as above, except add one 10-oz. package frozen spinach (partially thawed in the microwave). Spread some on each layer. Adds 10 calories and 2 grams of carbohydrate.

LASAGNA (MEATLESS VERSION)

Make the same as above, except omit the meat and substitute 2 low sodium beef bouillon cubes, or 2 tsp. dissolved in 1/2 cup boiling water, for the 1/4 cup water.

Nutrients per serving:		Exchanges:	
Calories	291	Bread	3
Fat	2g	Vegetable	2
Cholesterol	4mg		
Carbohydrate	54g		
Sodium	243mg		

SPAGHETTI AND MEATBALL EXCHANGE

1 cup spaghetti noodles = 2 breads
1 oz. hamburger meatball = 1 medium-fat meat
1/2 cup tomato sauce = 2 vegetables
1 cup lasagna = 1½ breads + 2 high-fat meats + 2 fats
1 cup ravioli = 2 breads + 1 high-fat meat + 1 vegetable
1/8 of pizza (14″ diameter) = 1½ breads + 1 high-fat meat

ONE-DISH SUPPER/MACARONI AND BEEF

1 cup elbow macaroni
1 lb. lean ground beef
1 cup diced onion
1 clove garlic, mashed
2 Tbs. oil
1/2 tsp. Italian seasoning
1/4 tsp. black pepper
1/2 tsp. salt substitute
1 (8-oz.) can tomato sauce (no salt added type)
1 cup low-sodium catsup
1 (8-oz.) can mushroom stems and pieces, drained
2 Tbs. Worcestershire sauce

Cook the macaroni in boiling water. Drain and set aside. Sauté the meat, onion, and garlic in oil until the meat loses its pink color and onions are tender. Add seasonings, pepper, tomato sauce, catsup, mushrooms, Worcestershire sauce. Bring mixture to a boil and then simmer gently for about 5 minutes. Mix in the cooked macaroni and simmer for 5 more minutes. Serves 8.

Note: May replace mushrooms with cream of celery soup. May use few shakes of garlic powder in place of garlic clove (up to 1/2 tsp.). May omit 1 Tbs. Worcestershire sauce if desired. May omit catsup, but nutrients are figured with it.

Nutrients per serving:		Exchanges:	
Calories	215	Bread	1
Fat	12g	Meat	1 1/2
Cholesterol	37mg	Vegetable	1
Carbohydrate	16g	Fat	1/2
Sodium	39mg		

Add 1/2 tsp. cooking oil to boiling water before adding pasta. Stir ocassionally; drain when done. Your pasta won't stick together.

BEEF-CARROT-CORN CASSEROLE

1 cup carrots, sliced
1/2 cup green beans
1 onion, diced
1/2 lb. lean ground beef
1 (15-oz.) can tomato sauce (Hunt's No Salt Added)

Cook the carrots and green beans in water until crisp tender. Brown the onion and ground beef. Drain them in a colander, then add carrots, green beans, and tomato sauce. Bake in oven or heat in microwave until heated through. Makes about 4 (1 cup) servings.

Nutrients per serving:		Exchanges:	
Calories	174	Meat	2
Fat	8g	Vegetable	2
Cholesterol	37mg		
Carbohydrate	9g		
Sodium	143mg		

STUFFED CABBAGE

1 head cabbage
1 lb. lean ground beef
1/2 cup finely chopped onion
1 egg
1 tsp. salt substitute
1 tsp. pepper (optional)
1 Tbs. paprika
1 cup raw rice
2 cups tomato juice (low-sodium)
3 cups water

Core cabbage and place in a pot with enough boiling water to cover it. Cook until the leaves wilt enough to roll. Mix ground beef, onion, egg, seasonings, and rice. Take cabbage out and fill each leaf with rice mixture (about 2 to 3 Tbs.) and roll up. Secure with toothpicks. Place in large pan with tomato juice and water. Simmer until rice is done (about 30 minutes). Serves 5.

Nutrients per serving:		Exchanges:	
Calories	364	Bread	2
Fat	14g	Meat	3
Cholesterol	114mg	Vegetable	1
Carbohydrate	37g		
Sodium	100mg		

To remove garlic odor from your hands, rub them with coffee grounds and rinse.

MARINATED BEEF SHISHKABOBS

- 1 small pot roast (about 2 lbs.) or large sirloin steak (about 1 1/2 lbs.), cut into 15 1-inch cubes
- 1/2 bottle cocktail onions (3 1/2 oz. size)
- 1 (2 1/2-oz.) bottle button mushrooms or 15 fresh ones
- 1 green pepper, cut into 15 (1 1/2-inch) squares

Marinade

- 1 cup burgundy wine
- 2 tsp. Worcestershire sauce
- 2 cloves garlic, or 1 tsp. garlic powder
- 1 cup vegetable oil
- 1/4 cup catsup
- 2 tsp. sugar
- 1 tsp. monosodium glutamate (Accent)
- 2 Tbs. vinegar
- 1 tsp. marjoram leaves
- 1 tsp. rosemary leaves

Mix marinade and put in baking pan with deep sides. Place a meat cube on wooden or metal skewers. Add a square of green pepper, a cocktail onion, and a mushroom cap. Let sit in marinade 1 day. Baste with marinade occasionally. Broil until meat is done. Serve hot. Makes 5 servings of 3 shishkabobs each.

Nutrients per serving:		Exchanges:	
Calories	390	Meat	3
Fat	30g	Vegetable	1
Cholesterol	70mg	Fat	3
Carbohydrate	6g		
Sodium	72mg		

Note: For hors d'oeuvres see recipe for Marinated Shishkabobs in the appetizer section.

A MEAL BY ITSELF

1 lb. lean ground meat
1 onion, chopped (1/2 cup)
1 can pork & beans
1 tsp. margarine
1 cup Ranch Style beans
1/4 cup catsup
1 Tbs. mustard
1 Tbs. brown SugarTwin

Brown meat and onion in margarine. Add all other ingredients and simmer in covered pan. Serves 8.

Nutrients per serving:		Exchanges:	
Calories	270	Bread	$1^1/_2$
Fat	1g	Meat	2
Cholesterol	37mg	Vegetable	1
Carbohydrate	28g		
Sodium	307mg		

GOOLASH

2 cups raw macaroni
1/2 lb. lean ground beef
1 med. onion, chopped
1/4 tsp. garlic powder
2 (4-oz.) cans Hunt's No Salt Added Tomato Sauce
1 cup Hunt's Catsup (low-salt)

Cook macaroni in boiling water for 7 minutes. Brown ground beef and onions; drain well. Add macaroni and other ingredients. Cover and simmer until well mixed and hot. Yields 8 (1-cup) servings.

Nutrients per serving:		Exchanges:	
Calories	198	Bread	1
Fat	6g	Meat	1
Cholesterol	24mg	Fat	1/2
Carbohydrate	16g		
Sodium	135mg		

PEPPER STEAK

1 lb. round steak (1/4 to 1/2-inch thick)
2 Tbs. Kikkoman Lite Soy Sauce
2 tsp. cornstarch
1 green pepper (cut into 8 sections)
2 cups water or more

Cut the round steak in long strips, then brown in soy sauce. Add green pepper. (If you want a more colorful dish, use red pepper or both colors. You can also use a cheaper cut of meat, but trim the fat.)

Mix cornstarch in 1 cup of cold water; pour over steak. (Use heavy cast-iron skillet.) Add the rest of the water and simmer for at least an hour. Check every few minutes to make sure the steak is not sticking. If necessary, add more water (1/2 cup at a time). This is good with rice or egg noodles. Serves 6.

Nutrients per serving:		Exchanges:	
Calories	126	Meat	1
Fat	4g	Vegetable	1
Cholesterol	46mg		
Carbohydrate	4g		
Sodium	241mg		

Drain browned hamburger in a colander or on a plate lined with several paper towels before adding other ingredients.

BARBECUE BEEF ROAST

Roast of beef (3 oz. per person; chuck or round, trim off fat)
1 Tbs. Woody's BarBQ Sauce (14 calories, 2 carb., 130 sod.)

Brown both sides of meat on grill. Place on foil. Brush both sides with sauce. Wrap and seal edges of foil. Set away from flame and cook for 1½ hours. Cooked portion equals 2-oz. serving.

Nutrients per serving:		Exchanges:	
Calories	189	Meat	2
Fat	8g		
Cholesterol	75mg		
Carbohydrate	2g		
Sodium	170mg		

NESTING LAMB

Lamb:

1 lb. ground lamb
1 medium onion, chopped
1 Tbs. oil
Salt and pepper to taste

Brown lamb and chopped onion in oil. Salt and pepper to taste. Drain. Place on top of nest of butternut squash.

Nest:

1 butternut squash

Place peeled squash in saucepan. Cover with water and boil until soft. Drain and mash. Add pepper and butter flavoring to taste. Serves 5.

Nutrients per serving:		Exchanges:	
Calories	220	Meat	2
Fat	21g	Vegetable	1
Cholesterol	89mg	Fat	2
Carbohydrate	3g		
Sodium	71mg		

LAMB BURRITOS

1 flour tortilla
2 Tbs. refried beans
2 Tbs. ground lamb
1 Tbs. shredded cheddar cheese
Shredded lettuce

Warm tortilla. Spread refried beans down the middle. Add meat, cheese, and lettuce. Roll up to eat. Serves 1. This is a great way to use any leftover lamb or ground beef.

Nutrients per serving:		Exchanges:	
Calories	230	Bread	$1\frac{1}{3}$
Fat	14g	Meat	2
Cholesterol	77mg	Fat	1
Carbohydrate	19g		
Sodium	252mg		

OLD WEST PORK CHOPS

6 pork chops (about 3 lbs.)
1 large onion, cut in 6 slices
2 tsp. chili powder
1 fresh green pepper, chopped
1 cup uncooked rice
2 (8-oz.) cans tomato sauce, Hunt's No Salt Added
1 1/4 cups water
1 tsp. No Salt salt

Rub pan with fat on chops to prevent sticking, then trim off fat. Brown chops well on both sides. Remove. Brown onion slices on both sides in same pan for 2 minutes. Remove. Stir in chili powder. Add green peppers, rice, tomato sauce, water, and salt. Heat to boiling. Pour into a shallow baking dish. Arrange browned chops over rice and place an onion slice on each one. Bake in oven at 375 degrees for 1 hour or until the liquid is absorbed. Serves 6.

Nutrients per serving:		Exchanges:	
Calories	326	Bread	2
Fat	11g	Meat	2 1/2
Cholesterol	72mg	Vegetable	1
Carbohydrate	33g		
Sodium	84mg		

Spices add flavor without calories!

PITA PIZZA

2/3 cup Hunt's Low Sodium Catsup
1/8 tsp. garlic powder
1 tsp. oregano
4 whole wheat pita pocket breads, split
1/3 cup green pepper, cut in strips
3 tsp. chopped onion
4 oz. mozzarella cheese, shredded
1 oz. pepperoni slices

Mix catsup, garlic powder, and oregano. Spread on pita pocket breads. Sprinkle with green pepper, onion, and cheese. Add pepperoni if desired.

Bake at 400 for 7–10 minutes. Makes 4 servings.

Nutrients per serving:		Exchanges:	
Calories	190	Bread	1
Fat	7g	Meat	1
Cholesterol	24mg	Vegetable	1
Carbohydrate	18g		
Sodium	134mg		

WILD RICE AND VENISON CHOPS

*6 venison chops
2 Tbs. margarine
1 pkg. long grain wild rice (6 oz.)
1 cup chopped onion
1 cup chopped celery
1 can Campbell's Special Request Cream of Mushroom soup (or cream of chicken)
2½ cups water
1/4 cup chopped pimiento
1/2 tsp. No Salt salt

Brown chops on one side in 1 Tbs. margarine. Remove chops and add remaining 1 Tbs. margarine to pan. Brown onion and celery. Add remaining ingredients and mix. Pour this mixture in 2-qt. baking dish or 9 x 13-inch pan. Arrange chops, brown side up, on mixture. Cover with aluminum foil, crimping it to edges of pan. Bake at 375 until chops are done and most of liquid is absorbed, about 1 hour. Serves 6. Do not let venison (or quail) dry out. Add water if needed.

**Note:* Using pork chops will increase the calories and fat. Using chicken or quail will decrease the calories and fat.

Nutrients per serving:		Exchanges:	
Calories	155	Bread	1
Fat	10g	Meat	2
Cholesterol	28mg		
Carbohydrate	11g		
Sodium	228mg		

HAM 'N SPAGHETTI

1 cup boneless ham (diced)
4 cups cooked spaghetti
1 cup light sour cream
2 Tbs. melted margarine
2 Tbs. green onion, chopped
3/4 cup cheese

Combine ingredients and toss lightly to coat noodles. Turn into 1 1/2-qt. casserole. Cover and bake 20 minutes at 350 degrees or until thoroughly heated. Serves 4. Good with a salad.

Nutrients per serving:		Exchanges:	
Calories	351	Bread	2
Fat	18g	Meat	2
Cholesterol	34mg	Fat	2
Carbohydrate	35g		
Sodium	155mg		

HAM AND CORN AU GRATIN

- 1 cup diced, cooked ham
- 2 1/2 cups cooked whole kernel corn
- 2 Tbs. grated onion
- 1/4 cup finely chopped green pepper
- 1 1/2 cups white sauce (see below)
- 1/2 tsp. dry mustard
- 1/2 cup grated cheese
- 1/2 cup breadcrumbs

Layer the ham, corn, grated onion, and pepper in greased 1 1/2-qt. casserole. Combine the white sauce and dry mustard and pour over all. Mix grated cheese and breadcrumbs and sprinkle on top. Bake at 375 for 25 minutes until browned. Serves 6.

White Sauce:

- 1/2 cup skim milk
- 1/4 tsp. No Salt salt
- 1 Tbs. flour (can use 1/2 Tbs. cornstarch for 13 less calories)

Mix flour with 2 Tbs. cold skim milk until all lumps are gone. Add salt, and cook over medium heat, stirring constantly until thickened. Makes 1/2 cup.

Nutrients per serving:	Whole Recipe	Just Sauce
Calories	192	69
Fat	3g	0
Cholesterol	23mg	2mg
Carbohydrate	19g	12g
Sodium	76mg	67mg

Exchanges: Whole Recipe		Just Sauce	
Bread	1	Milk	1
Meat	1		
Vegetable	1		

APPLE HAM CASSEROLE

1 Tbs. fresh lemon juice
2 small apples, cored, peeled, diced
1/3 cup brown SugarTwin
1/2 tsp. grated orange peel
2 Tbs. flour
1½ cups cooked ham, diced

Grease a 1½-qt. casserole. Sprinkle lemon juice over apples. Mix brown SugarTwin, orange peel, and flour. Mix this with ham and apples and place in casserole. Bake, uncovered, at 350 degrees for 30–35 minutes. Four (3/4-cup) servings.

Note: Heart patients should limit themselves to 800 mg. sodium per meal and not eat more than 1 serving of this dish.

Nutrients per serving:	
Calories	179
Fat	3g
Cholesterol	28mg
Carbohydrate	10g
Sodium	768mg

Exchanges:	
Bread	1/2
Meat	1½
Fruit	1/2

STUFFED VEAL ROLLS

4 veal cutlets (1 lb.) about 1/4-inch thick
2 Tbs. chopped onion
1/4 cup sliced mushrooms
1 Tbs. margarine
1 tsp. parsley flakes
1/8 tsp. garlic powder
1/4 tsp. No Salt salt
1/8 tsp. sage
1/8 tsp. pepper
1 cup fresh whole wheat breadcrumbs (about 2 slices)
Toothpicks
1 cup low-sodium broth or bouillon
2 tsp. flour
2 Tbs. water

Pound the cutlets until 1/8-inch thick. Sauté the onion and mushrooms in margarine in a small pan until lightly browned. Remove pan from heat and stir in parsley, seasonings, and crumbs. Divide stuffing among cutlets and spread on each. Roll up and fasten with toothpicks. Spray skillet with Pam and brown veal rolls on all sides. Add beef broth. Boil, then reduce heat and cover. Simmer 20–30 minutes or until tender. Remove veal rolls. Mix flour and water until all lumps are gone. Add to skillet and cook until thick, stirring constantly. Pour over veal. Makes 4 (3-oz.) servings.

Nutrients per serving:		Exchanges:	
Calories	230	Bread	1
Fat	14g	Meat	1
Cholesterol	80mg	Fat	2
Carbohydrate	10g		
Sodium	320mg		

FISH WITH WILD RICE

1½ lbs. fresh fish fillets (whitefish type)
1 tsp. salt substitute
1/4 tsp. pepper
1 cup sliced fresh mushrooms (about 1/4 lb.)
1/4 cup onion, chopped
1 Tbs. margarine
6 oz. Uncle Ben's Long Grain and Wild Rice, cooked with 1/2 tsp. salt substitute
1 Tbs. melted margarine

Cut fish into serving-size portions and sprinkle with salt substitute and pepper. Sauté mushrooms and onion in margarine until soft. Stir in rice. Place fish in baking dish and cover with rice mixture. Drizzle melted margarine on top of rice. Cover and bake at 350 for 20 minutes or until fish flakes easily. Serve 6 with sauce below.

Mushroom walnut sauce:

1 Tbs. minced onion
1 cup sliced fresh mushrooms (about 1/4 lb.)
2 Tbs. margarine
3 Tbs. flour
1/4 tsp. salt substitute
1/4 tsp. thyme
2 cups evaporated skim milk
1/4 cup toasted walnuts

Sauté onion and mushrooms in melted margarine until tender. Stir in flour, salt substitute, and thyme. Gradually mix in the evaporated milk. Cook over medium heat, stirring constantly. Add walnuts. Makes about 2½ cups sauce.

Nutrients per serving:		Exchanges:	
Calories	430	Bread	2
Fat	11g	Meat	3
Cholesterol	111mg	Milk	1/2
Carbohydrate	38g	Vegetable	1
Sodium	174mg		

SALMON TREAT

1 (7 1/2-oz.) can salmon
4 Tbs. Miracle Whip Light
1 pkg. Sweet 'N Low
1 apple, finely chopped
1/2 cup chopped pecans
1/2 cup chopped celery (optional)

Mix ingredients together. Chill and serve cold. Serves 4.

Nutrients per serving:		Exchanges:	
Calories	238	Meat	2
Fat	16g	Fruit	1
Cholesterol	21mg	Fat	1
Carbohydrate	12g		
Sodium	406mg		

SALMON LOAF

1 can (15 1/2-oz.) salmon
1/3 cup finely minced onion
2 Tbs. minced parsley
1 Tbs. lemon juice
1/4 tsp. No Salt salt
2 cups soft breadcrumbs
1/3 cup skim milk
1 egg
1 egg white
1/4 tsp. dill weed

Drain and flake salmon. Reserve 2 Tbs. liquid. Combine all ingredients and place in greased loaf pan. Bake at 350 degrees for 45 minutes. Makes 6 servings.

Nutrients per serving:		Exchanges:	
Calories	147	Bread	1/2
Fat	6g	Meat	1
Cholesterol	11mg		
Carbohydrate	6g		
Sodium	439mg		

SCALLOPED TUNA

1 cup soft breadcrumbs
1 1/2 cups skim milk
2 Tbs. margarine
1 egg
2 egg whites
1/2 tsp. salt substitute
1/4 tsp. pepper
1 small onion, minced
1 tsp. parsley flakes
1 (6 1/2 oz.) can water-packed tuna

Heat breadcrumbs with milk and margarine until margarine melts. Meanwhile beat egg and egg whites. Stir in salt, pepper, onion, parsley flakes, and tuna. Gradually stir in hot milk and crumbs. Place in casserole dish and bake at 350 for 25–30 minutes. Serves 5.

Nutrients per serving:	
Calories	165
Fat	10g
Cholesterol	72mg
Carbohydrate	14g
Sodium	452mg

Exchanges:	
Bread	1
Meat	1
Fat	1

Imitation mayonnaise has fewer calories, fat, cholesterol, carbohydrate, and sodium than light mayonnaise. Check the labels.

PEPPER'S TUNA CASSEROLE

1 (6 1/2-oz.) can water-packed tuna
1/2 cup onion, diced
1 (6-oz.) pkg. egg noodles
1 can light cream of mushroom soup
No Salt salt to taste
Pepper to taste
2 slices light sandwich cheese

Cook noodles; drain. Mix in all ingredients and top with the cheese. Bake at 350 degrees for about 45 minutes to 1 hour. Serves 8.

Nutrients per serving:		Exchanges:	
Calories	72	Meat	1
Fat	3g		
Cholesterol	5mg		
Carbohydrate	3g		
Sodium	146mg		

STUFFED FISH

- 1/2 cup chopped onion (1 small)
- 1 Tbs. Fleischmann's Margarine
- 3/4 tsp. garlic powder
- $1\frac{1}{2}$ cups whole wheat soft breadcrumbs (2 slices)
- 2 tsp. parsley flakes
- 2 Tbs. lemon juice, divided
- 1 tsp. grated lemon rind
- 2 Tbs. water
- 1/4 tsp. thyme, crushed
- 1/4 tsp. marjoram
- 1/8 tsp. pepper
- 1 lb. frozen perch fillets, thawed, cut in 6 equal-size pieces or $1\frac{1}{2}$ lbs. fresh fish, dressed, with bones removed but left whole with slit for stuffing

Preheat oven to 350 degrees. Cook onion in margarine until soft. Remove from heat and stir in garlic powder, breadcrumbs, parsley flakes, 1 Tbs. lemon juice, lemon rind, 2 Tbs. water, thyme, marjoram, and pepper. Spray baking dish with nonstick cooking spray or line with aluminum foil. Pound thawed frozen fish until flat enough to spread 3 pieces with stuffing and cover with 3 more pieces. For fresh fish, just place stuffing in slit. Secure fish together with toothpicks or skewers and place in baking dish. Sprinkle with lemon juice. Cover. Bake 25–35 minutes or until fish flakes. Makes 3 generous servings.

Nutrients per serving:		Exchanges:	
Calories	122	Bread	2/3
Fat	4g	Meat	1
Cholesterol	26mg		
Carbohydrate	10g		
Sodium	122mg		

FISH FLORENTINE

- 1 lb. fresh or frozen sole, perch or flounder
- 1 (10-oz.) pkg. frozen chopped spinach
- 3 lg. fresh mushrooms, sliced or 1 (4-oz.) can pieces, drained
- 1 Tbs. margarine or bacon fat
- 1 Tbs. bacon bits (real or imitation)
- 1/2 tsp. salt

Thaw fish; rinse and dry with paper towels. Pound until thin. Thaw spinach in package (poke holes in top with fork and microwave on high until thawed enough to drain and spread over fish). Sauté mushrooms in margarine or bacon fat. Mix spinach with bacon bits and salt. Spread over fish. Lay mushrooms on top of spinach. Roll fish up and secure with toothpicks.

Place in baking dish so each end (place where you finished rolling) is braced against side or bottom of dish. Bake covered in a 375-degree oven for 15–20 minutes or until fish flakes easily.

Or cook in microwave on high for 6–8 minutes. Cover with plastic wrap or glass cover and turn after cooking 3 minutes to even the effect of the microwaves, which may cook unevenly in some microwave ovens. Serves 4.

Nutrients per serving:	
Calories	136
Fat	5g
Cholesterol	60mg
Carbohydrate	3g
Sodium	488mg

Exchanges:	
Meat	1
Vegetable	1

CRABBY NOODLES

- 3 oz. medium egg noodles
- 4 cups boiling water
- 1 cup large fresh mushrooms, sliced 1/4-inch thick
- 1 Tbs. margarine
- 4 oz. Delicaseas Seastix (frozen, cooked imitation crabmeat)
- 3/4 cup evaporated milk
- 1 Tbs. lemon juice (bottled okay)
- 1 (8-oz.) Neufchatel cream cheese

Boil egg noodles in the water; drain well. Sauté the mushrooms in the margarine for a few minutes. Add the rest of the ingredients and heat through. Makes 5 (1-cup) servings.

Nutrients per serving:		Exchanges:	
Calories	184	Bread	1
Fat	10g	Meat	1
Cholesterol	64mg	Fat	1
Carbohydrate	13g		
Sodium	372mg		

Salads

GARDEN CHICKEN SALAD

2 cups cooked chicken, diced
2 cups broccoli, cut in flowerets
16 large green grape halves (or 24 small grapes)
4 Tbs. Kraft Reduced Calorie Buttermilk Dressing
2 Tbs. skim milk
2 tomatoes, cut up
4 lettuce leaves

Microwave broccoli with a little water for 5 minutes on high; drain and chill. Mix dressing with milk. Mix all ingredients except lettuce. Serve on lettuce leaf. Serves 4.

Nutrients per serving:	
Calories	215
Fat	5g
Cholesterol	62mg
Carbohydrate	10g
Sodium	164mg

Exchanges:	
Meat	2 1/2
Vegetable	1
Fruit	1/2

TUNA SALAD

1/2 cup low-calorie mayonnaise
1 Tbs. lemon juice
2 Tbs. chopped green onions (tops and all)
2 (6 1/2-oz.) cans water-packed tuna
1/2 cup chopped celery

Combine all ingredients and toss slightly before serving. Serve on a bed of shredded lettuce. Serves 6. (From Dr. Richard Berger.)

Nutrients per serving:		Exchanges:	
Calories	131	Meat	1
Fat	4g	Fat	1
Cholesterol	35mg		
Carbohydrate	1g		
Sodium	413mg		

Use tomato, lemon, or pickle juice (not sweet pickle juice) instead of salad dressing.

SELF-DRESSED SALAD

1 small tomato, diced
1 cucumber, diced
2 stalks celery, diced
3 radishes, diced
Pepper to taste
2 Tbs. lemon juice

Mix, seal in bowl, and refrigerate overnight. Juices mix to form a dressing. Serve 1/2 cup on lettuce leaf. Serves 2.

Nutrients per serving:		Exchanges:	
Calories	47	Vegetable	1
Fat	0g		
Cholesterol	0mg		
Carbohydrate	3g		
Sodium	35mg		

MEXICAN SALAD

Dressing:

1 cup lowfat yogurt, plain
3/4 cup Mild Chili Sauce (see below)
1/4 cup ginger ale or 7-Up (sugar-free)

Mix well and add ginger ale or 7-Up gradually. Refrigerate.

Salad:

1/2 lb. ground beef, cooked, drained
1 head iceberg lettuce

Line bowl with bite-size pieces of lettuce. Layer the following:

1 medium onion, chopped
2 medium tomatoes, peeled, diced
1 (1-lb.) can kidney beans, drained
2 cups (8-oz.) diet cheese, grated
1 cup tortilla chips, broken

Mild Chili Sauce:

1/3 cup green onions, thinly sliced
1 garlic clove, minced
1/4 tsp. hot chili paste
1/2 cup white vinegar
1/4 tsp. sesame oil

Combine all ingredients in a bowl and stir well. Store in refrigerator in airtight container. Yields about 2/3 cup. Top salad with 1 Tbs. dressing. Serves 6.

Nutrients per serving:	
Calories	286
Fat	16g
Cholesterol	54mg
Carbohydrate	15g
Sodium	349mg

Exchanges:	
Bread	1
Meat	2
Fat	1

LEMON/LIME GELATIN

1 (3-oz.) pkg. lemon gelatin (sugar-free)
1 (3-oz.) pkg. lime gelatin (sugar-free)

Dissolve in 2 cups of hot water. Chill until thick as a raw egg white.
Mix together and stir into thickened gelatin:

16 oz. cottage cheese (lowfat)
1/2 cup light mayonnaise
1 lg. can crushed pineapple (no sugar added), drained and rinsed in water
1 Tbs. horseradish
1/2 cup pecans, chopped

Spoon into parfait glasses and chill. Garnish with kiwi fruit. Serves 6.

Nutrients per serving:	
Calories	230
Fat	16g
Cholesterol	9mg
Carbohydrate	11g
Sodium	379mg

Exchanges:	
Meat (cottage cheese)	2
Milk	1/2
Fruit	1/2
Fat	1

COLA FRUIT SALAD

1 envelope unflavored gelatin
3 pkg. Equal (optional)
1/4 cup water (or fruit juice)
Juice of 1 lemon
1½ cups diet ginger ale or Diet Coke
1½ cups diced fruit (fresh, canned or frozen unsweetened; if you use fresh or frozen pineapple, gelatin won't get firm)

Mix gelatin with a little water in pan. Add rest of water and lemon juice. Cook over low heat, stirring constantly until gelatin dissolves. Remove from heat and stir in ginger ale. Chill until it's as thick as a raw egg white. Stir in fruit and chill until firm. Serves 4.

Nutrients per serving:		Exchanges:	
Calories	50	Fruit	1
Fat	0		
Cholesterol	0		
Carbohydrate	12g		
Sodium	28mg		

FRESH kiwi fruit, as well as FRESH pineapple juice and pulp, contain enzymes that prevent gelatin from setting. Never use them in gelatin molds. Kiwi fruit has an enzyme that causes composition changes when used with milk, but it makes a delicious topping.

COCKTAIL DELIGHT

1 lg. can fruit cocktail in own juice, drained and rinsed with water
1 banana, sliced thinly
1 apple, diced
1/2 sm. pkg. orange gelatin (sugar-free)

Mix together and chill for an hour before serving. Serves 4.

Nutrients per serving:		Exchanges:	
Calories	65	Fruit	1
Fat	0		
Cholesterol	0mg		
Carbohydrate	17g		
Sodium	9mg		

COKE SALAD

1/2 cup pineapple juice
1 Tbsp. lemon juice
1 cup Diet Coke
1 (3-oz.) pkg. Cherry Jell-o (sugar-free)
8 oz. can crushed pineapple (unsweetened, well drained)
1 cup frozen cherries halved (sugar-free)
1/4 cup chopped pecans

Heat pineapple juice, lemon juice, and 1/2 cup of water until almost boiling. Stir in Jell-o until dissolved. Let cool slightly, then add fruit, nuts, and cold Coke. (Diet Coke loses its sweetness if it gets hot.) Chill. Serves 6. If you are short on pineapple juice, make up the difference with water.

Nutrients per serving:		Exchanges:	
Calories	53.8	Fruit	1/2
Fat	3g	Fat	1/2
Cholesterol	0		
Carbohydrate	6.7g		
Sodium	0		

GREAT SPICED PEACHES

1 small cinnamon stick
1/2 tsp. allspice
1 tsp. cloves
1 cup vinegar
1 can peach halves (no sugar added), drained (save juice)

Put peach juice in a large pan with spices and vinegar. Simmer 30 minutes. Pour over peaches. Chill overnight. Serves 6.

Nutrients per serving:		Exchanges:	
Calories	17	Fruit	1/2
Fat	7g		
Cholesterol	0		
Carbohydrate	9g		
Sodium	3mg		

GRAPEFRUIT SUPREME

- 4 sm. grapefruits
- 1 cup mandarin orange, segmented
- 1 cup unpeeled apples, diced
- 1 cup seedless green or tokay grapes, halved
- 1 cup raspberry or cherry sugarfree yogurt

Cut each grapefruit in half. Cut around edges and membranes to remove grapefruit sections; drain sections. Remove membrane from shells; reserve shells. With scissors, scallop edges of shells. Mix all fruits. Fill each shell with 1 cup fruit mixture. Chill. Just before serving, top each shell with 1 Tbs. yogurt. Serves 8.

Nutrients per serving:		Exchanges:	
Calories	99	Fruit	1 1/4
Fat	0g		
Cholesterol	1mg		
Carbohydrate	18g		
Sodium	17mg		

FRESH FRUIT SALAD

- 2 red delicious apples, diced
- 2 golden delicious apples, diced
- 1 cup seedless grapes
- 2 bananas, sliced
- 2 fresh peaches, sliced
- 1/4 cup chopped pecans
- 1/2 box sugar-free orange Jell-o

Mix fruits and nuts in bowl. Sprinkle dry Jell-o over mixture; cover and chill for 2 or 3 hours. Allow to steep in own juices. Serves 8.

Note: You may use sugar-free fruit cocktail and add any fresh or canned fruit you desire. Excellent for potluck luncheons.

Nutrients per serving:		Exchanges:	
Calories	118	Fruit	1 1/3
Fat	5g		
Cholesterol	0mg		
Carbohydrate	19g		
Sodium	2mg		

APPLE NOTES

1 lb. of apples consists of: 4 small apples, or 3 medium apples, or 2 large apples
1 lb. of apples = 3 cups diced apples
1 lb. of apples = 2 3/4 cups sliced apples
2 medium apples yield 1 cup grated apples

7-UP SALAD

1 (8-oz.) can crushed pineapple (no sugar added)
1 lg. pkg. sugar-free lime Jell-o
1 (12-oz.) bottle sugar-free 7-Up
1 (8-oz.) pkg. light cream cheese
1 cup Lite Cool Whip
1/2 cup flaked coconut
1/2 cup chopped pecans

Drain pineapple and reserve the juice. Mix Jell-o with 1/2 of the required boiling water (1 cup). When completely dissolved, add chilled 7-Up and place in 9 x 9-inch dish and refrigerate.

Blend juice from pineapple and cream cheese. When Jell-o mix is nearly set but still slightly runny, add cream cheese-juice mixture. Beat until smooth. Add Cool Whip and fold in until smooth. Add one at a time, folding in evenly: crushed pineapple, coconut, and pecans. Chill until set. Serves 8.

Nutrients per serving:	
Calories	199
Fat	14g
Cholesterol	25mg
Carbohydrate	9g
Sodium	154mg

Exchanges:	
Fruit	1/2
Fat	3

MARINATED EGGPLANT SALAD

1/2 cup olive oil (4-oz.)
1/4 cup vinegar
1/2 tsp. garlic powder
1/2 onion, finely chopped
1 medium green pepper, cut in 2-inch strips
1/2 tsp. thyme
1/4 tsp. salt substitute
1 large eggplant, sliced and cut in chunks

Mix all ingredients and marinate 8 hours. Drain before serving on lettuce leaf. Serves 8.

Nutrients per serving:		Exchanges:	
Calories	134	Vegetable	1
Fat	10g	Fat	2
Cholesterol	—		
Carbohydrate	3.2g		
Sodium	135mg		

SUMMER SALAD

1 (3-oz.) pkg. sugar-free lemon Jell-o
1½ cups boiling water
1/4 tsp. salt substitute
1 cup diced cucumbers
2 Tbs. diced green pepper
2 Tbs. chopped pimiento
1 Tbs. diced onion
2 cups diced celery

Dissolve Jell-o in boiling water; add salt. Place in refrigerator until slightly congealed. Add vegetables. Pour in oiled mold. Chill. Serves 2.

Nutrients per serving:		Exchanges:	
Calories	56	Vegetable	2
Fat	0		
Cholesterol	0		
Carbohydrate	11g		
Sodium	142mg		

SALMON TREAT

1 (7½-oz.) can salmon
4 Tbs. light mayonnaise
1 pkg. Sweet 'n Low
1 large apple, finely chopped
1/2 cup chopped pecans
1/2 cup chopped celery (optional)

Mix ingredients together; chill and serve cold. Serves 4.

Nutrients per serving:		Exchanges:	
Calories	125	Meat	2
Fat	12g	Fruit	1/2
Cholesterol	30g	Fat	1/2
Carbohydrate	6g		
Sodium	38mg		

FAST POTATO SALAD (Microwave)

24 oz. frozen hash brown potatoes
4 slices bacon
1 sm. chopped onion
2 tsp. Equal (1 pkg.)
1 tsp. flour
1 tsp. instant beef bouillon (or 1 cube)
1 tsp. salt substitute
2 Tbs. vinegar
1/2 cup water
1 tsp. chopped chives

In a 2-qt. glass casserole, microwave potatoes on high for 9–10 minutes until steaming hot. Set aside.

Place bacon in $1\frac{1}{2}$-qt. glass casserole. Cover with paper towel. Microwave on high 4 to 5 minutes until crisp. Remove bacon and set aside. Add onions to bacon drippings. Microwave on high $2\frac{1}{2}$ to 3 minutes or until tender. Stir in Equal, flour, bouillon, salt substitute, vinegar, and water. Microwave on high 2–3 minutes until mixture boils, stirring once. Stir in crumbled bacon, potatoes, and chives. Cover with plastic wrap. Microwave on high 4 to 5 minutes until heated thoroughly. Serves 6.

Nutrients per serving:		Exchanges:	
Calories	251	Bread	1
Fat	15g	Meat	1
Cholesterol	11mg	Vegetable	2
Carbohydrate	24g	Fat	2
Sodium	233mg		

COLD POTATO SALAD

1 cup Light Miracle Whip
1/2 tsp. celery seed
1/2 tsp. salt substitute
1/8 tsp. black pepper
4 cups cooked (about 6) potatoes, cubed
2 hard-boiled eggs, chopped
1/2 cup chopped onion
1/2 cup chopped celery
1/2 cup chopped pickles

Mix Miracle Whip, celery seed, salt substitute, and pepper in large bowl. Then add the potatoes, eggs, onion, celery, and pickle. Stir to coat thoroughly. Chill. Serves 6.

Nutrients per serving:		Exchanges:	
Calories	240	Bread	2 1/2
Fat	8g	Vegetable	1
Cholesterol	86mg	Fat	1 1/2
Carbohydrate	39g		
Sodium	350mg		

LEMON GAZPACHO

1 medium tomato, chopped
1/2 cup cucumber, diced
1/4 cup green pepper or celery, chopped
2 scallions, chopped
2 Tbs. vinegar
1/4 tsp. No Salt salt
Dash of pepper
1 (3-oz.) pkg. lemon Jell-o, sugar-free
3/4 cup boiling water
1/2 cup ice cubes and water

Combine vegetables, vinegar, salt, and pepper; set aside. Dissolve gelatin in boiling water. Add cold water to ice cubes to make 1 1/4 cups; add to gelatin. Stir until slightly thickened. Remove unmelted ice. Add vegetable mixture. Chill until thickened, about 5 minutes. Pour into individual dishes. Chill, soft set in 30 minutes. Garnish with vegetables. Serves 6.

Nutrients per serving:		Exchanges:	
Calories	17	Vegetable	1
Fat	0		
Cholesterol	0		
Carbohydrate	3g		
Sodium	24mg		

CUCUMBER GAZPACHO

- 2 slices whole wheat bread, crumbled
- 2 Tbs. white vinegar
- 2 Tbs. safflower oil
- 1/8 tsp. garlic powder
- 1 cup cucumber, diced
- 1 Tbs. green onion, finely sliced
- 3 cups tomatoes, peeled, chopped
- 1 cup tomato juice

Mix crumbs, vinegar, oil and garlic powder into a smooth paste. Mix in other ingredients. Chill 4 hours. Serves 6.

Nutrients per serving:		Exchanges:	
Calories	108	Bread	1/2
Fat	5g	Vegetable	1
Cholesterol	0	Fat	1
Carbohydrate	13g		
Sodium	84mg		

ORANGE CONFETTI

- 1 (3-oz.) pkg. orange Jell-o (sugar-free)
- 3/4 cup boiling water
- 1/4 cup cold water
- 3–4 ice cubes
- 1/2 cup shredded carrots
- 1/2 cup shredded cabbage

Dissolve gelatin in boiling water. Combine water and ice cubes to equal 1 cup. Add to gelatin, stirring until slightly thickened. Remove any unmelted ice. Add carrots and cabbage. Chill until set, about 10 minutes. Serves 5.

Nutrients per serving:		Exchanges:	
Calories	10	Vegetables	2
Fat	0		
Cholesterol	0		
Carbohydrate	10g		
Sodium	15mg		

LIGHT PERFECTION SALAD

1 envelope unflavored gelatin
1/4 tsp. No Salt salt
$1\frac{1}{4}$ cups water
1/4 cup vinegar
6 pkg. Equal
1 Tbs. lemon juice (bottled okay)
1/2 cup finely shredded cabbage
1 cup chopped celery
or
1/2 cup chopped cucumbers and 1 small chopped onion (version #1)
or
1/2 cup chopped raw cauliflower and 2 Tbs. minced green pepper (version #2)
or
1 pimiento, minced, or 2 Tbs. minced sweet red or green pepper (version #3)

Mix gelatin with salt in a pan. Stir in 1/2 cup of the water and heat over medium heat until gelatin dissolves. Take off heat and stir in 3/4 cup water, vinegar, Equal, and lemon juice. Chill until mixture is as thick as a raw egg white. Stir in chopped vegetables. Pour into a 2-cup mold and chill until firm. Serves 4.

Nutrients per serving:

	#1	#2	#3
Calories	28	30	27
Fat	0	0	0
Cholesterol	0	0	0
Carbohydrate	4g	5.5g	5g
Sodium	55mg	56mg	57mg

Exchanges:

Vegetable	1

STEWART'S SALAD

1st layer:
2 (3-oz.) pkg. sugar-free lemon Jell-o (prepared)
Few drops green food coloring
1 (20-oz.) can crushed pineapple in own juice, drained

2nd layer:
1 (8-oz) pkg. softened lite cream cheese
*1 pkg. Lite Dream Whip (make with skim milk)

3rd layer:

1 cup pineapple juice, unsweetened
2 tsp. flour
2 egg yolks
16 pkg. Equal

Mix Jell-o, food coloring, and drained pineapple. Pour into a 9 x 13-inch pan and chill until firm. Blend the cream cheese and Dream Whip together. Spread over chilled Jell-o layer. Chill. Cook third layer ingredients until thick; then cool. Drop by spoonfuls over second layer and spread carefully. Keep chilled until ready to serve. Serves 12.

* May use 8 oz. Lite Cool Whip.

Nutrients per serving:	Equal	Exchanges:	
Calories	114	Fruit	1
Fat	5g	Fat	1/2
Cholesterol	42mg		
Carbohydrate	12g		
Sodium	129mg		

Add a little skim milk to regular or 2% milk and keep increasing the amount until you get used to drinking plain skim milk.

Snacks

CINNAMON TOAST

Cinnamon to taste
1 pkg. Equal
1 slice light bread (40 calories per slice)
1 tsp. Fleischmann's Margarine

Mix cinnamon and Equal together. Toast bread. Spread margarine on one side and sprinkle with cinnamon mixture. Serves 1.

Nutrients per slice:		Exchanges:	
Calories	48	Bread	1/2
Fat	4g	Fat	1
Cholesterol	—		
Carbohydrate	7g		
Sodium	115mg		

CINNAMON MUFFIN

1 pkg. Equal
Cinnamon to taste
1/2 English muffin
1 tsp. Fleischmann's Margarine

Mix Equal and cinnamon. Toast one side of muffin. Spread other side with margarine, then sprinkle with cinnamon mixture. Toast. Serves 1.

Nutrients per slice:		Exchanges:	
Calories	104	Bread	1
Fat	5g	Fat	1
Cholesterol	—		
Carbohydrate	14g		
Sodium	100mg		

Note: This makes a nice midmorning snack at the office when your friends are gobbling those sweet rolls with their coffee.

RAISIN/CINNAMON TOAST

Cinnamon to taste
1 pkg. Equal
1 slice raisin bread
1 tsp. Fleischmann's Margarine

Mix cinnamon and Equal together. Toast bread. Spread with margarine and sprinkle with cinnamon/Equal mixture. Serves 1.

Nutrients per slice:		Exchanges:	
Calories	103	Bread	1
Fat	5g	Fat	1
Cholesterol	—		
Carbohydrate	13g		
Sodium	92mg		

PITA POCKET CRISPS

2 whole wheat pita pocket breads (6–7 inches in diameter)
2 Tbs. Fleischmann's Margarine
1/2 tsp. oregano
1/8 tsp. rubbed thyme
1/8 tsp. garlic powder
2 tsp. sesame seeds

Slit each pocket bread into 2 flat circles. Melt margarine and mix in spices (not sesame seeds). With a pastry brush, spread herb butter on bread. Sprinkle with sesame seeds. Cut each circle into 8 wedges. Bake on ungreased cookie sheet at 350 degrees for about 5 minutes or until crisp and slightly brown. Be careful not to overcook. Makes 8 servings of 4 pieces each.

Nutrients per serving:		Exchanges:	
Calories	87	Bread	1/2
Fat	4.5g	Fat	1
Cholesterol	—		
Carbohydrate	8g		
Sodium	45mg		

APPLE WHIZ

3 pkg. Equal
Cinnamon to taste (about 1/8 tsp.)
1 small apple

Mix Equal and cinnamon together. Peel apple if desired. Slice and spread on microwavable plate. Sprinkle with Equal/cinnamon mixture. Cook on high in microwave for 1 minute. Cover with a paper napkin and let set 1 minute. Serves 1.

Nutrients per serving:		Exchanges:	
Calories	93	Fruit	1 1/2
Fat	—		
Cholesterol	0		
Carbohydrate	24g		
Sodium	—		

STRAWBERRY SWEET TREATS

1 can Hungry Jack Buttermilk Biscuits (10 ct.)
3 1/3 Tbs. Strawberry Simply Fruit

Flatten biscuits into about 3-inch circles. Spread each with one teaspoon Simply Fruit and bake as directed on biscuit can. Serves 10.

Note: For variety try other Smucker's Simply Fruits.

Nutrients per biscuit:		Exchanges:	
Calories	106	Bread	1/2
Fat	4g	Fat	1
Cholesterol	0	Fruit	1/2
Carbohydrate	16g		
Sodium	300mg		

SNACK TIPS

Unsalted popcorn and diet soda make an excellent evening snack.

Use the various flavors of Molly McButter to flavor air popped popcorn.

Eat a slice of cucumber marinated in vinegar to kill a craving for sweets.

Refrigerate carrot and celery sticks in ice water to retain their crispness. Keep some cut up in the refrigerator, ready for that "snack attack" feeling.

Soups

STEAK SOUP

- 1/2 lb. ground beef
- 2 medium onions, chopped
- $1^1/_2$ cups sliced carrots (3 large)
- 2 cups water
- 2 Tbs. margarine
- 8 Tbs. cornstarch
- 1/2 cup cold water
- 1 (15-oz.) can Hunt's Tomato Sauce (low-salt)
- 6 tsp. beef bouillon crystals (low-salt)
- 1/2 tsp. black pepper
- 1 (10-oz.) package frozen lima beans, baby or Fordhook
- 6 cups water

Brown ground beef and chopped onions. Drain grease off. Boil meat with carrots in water for 10 minutes. Melt margarine in frying pan and mix in 2 Tbs. cornstarch. In separate bowl mix remaining 6 Tbs. cornstarch and 1/2 cup cold water with fork until all lumps are dissolved. Add both cornstarch mixtures and rest of ingredients to meat and onions. Add 6 cups water and simmer 20 minutes. It's better if you cook until it is quite thick (stir often). However, you have to add water when reheating or it will stick to the bottom of pan and burn. Serves 8.

Nutrients per serving:	
Calories	213
Fat	10g
Cholesterol	25mg
Carbohydrate	27g
Sodium	98mg

Exchanges:	
Bread	$1^1/_2$
Meat	1
Vegetable	1
Fat	1

If made with one pound of ground beef, add 163 calories, 25 grams cholesterol and 6 grams fat (plus 1 meat and 1 fat exchange) for each serving.

OXTAIL SOUP

1 pkg. oxtail (15 oz.)
2 cans tomatoes (salt-free)
1/2 cup celery
1/2 tsp. sugar substitute
1/2 cup catsup
1 pkg. frozen vegetables
2 large potatoes, cubed
1/2 Tbs. hot sauce
1/4 stick margarine
Salt and pepper to taste

Pressure cook oxtail; cut off fat, then combine meat with rest of ingredients. Heat and eat. Serves 6.

Nutrients per serving:	
Calories	276
Fat	11g
Cholesterol	31mg
Carbohydrate	23g
Sodium	67mg

Exchanges:	
Bread	1
Meat	2
Vegetable	1 1/2
Fat	1/2

NINE BEAN SOUP

Buy 1 lb. of each of the following dried beans, etc.; mix well and divide into 10 (2-cup) packages. (Save the bags beans come in to store mixed beans.)

Barley Pearls
Black Beans
Red Beans
Pinto Beans
Navy Beans
Great Northern Beans
Lentils
Split Peas
Black-Eyed Peas

Directions:

2 cups mixed beans
2 qts. water
2 large onions, chopped
1/2 lb. ground beef or diced ham or chicken
1/2 tsp. garlic powder
1/2 tsp. No Salt salt
2 (15-oz.) cans tomato sauce, low-sodium type

Wash and soak the beans for 5 hours. Cook with chopped onions for an hour. Brown ground beef and drain off grease. Add the rest of the ingredients to soup and cook for 1/2 hour more, or until slightly thick. Tastes good reheated but scorches easily, so add water and stir carefully or heat in bowls in the microwave. Makes 8–10 servings. (You can make it without meat and substitute about 6 bouillon cubes for the meat and the salt, but it has less flavor and more sodium unless you use the low-sodium bouillon.) Yields 10 servings.

Nutrients per serving:

Made with:	Bouillon	Beef	Chicken
Calories	128	153	135
Fat	2g	5g	1g
Cholesterol	0	20mg	8mg
Carbohydrate	15g	15g	15g
Sodium	508mg	526mg	525mg

Exchanges:

	1 bread	1 bread	1 bread
		1 meat	1 meat

Note: Although the grams of carbohydrate are the same in all, 1 bread exchange should only have 80 calories, so the nonmeat version is counted as 1½ breads.

CREAMY POTATO SOUP

2½ cups potatoes, peeled, cut up
1 medium onion, chopped
3 cups boiling water
3/4 tsp. No Salt salt
1 cup nonfat dry milk
2 Tbs. cornstarch (3 Tbs. makes it quite thick)
1½ cups cold water
1 tsp. Molly McButter (powdered butter substitute)
Pepper to taste (optional)
Parsley flakes (optional)

Cook potatoes and onion in boiling water without salt until potatoes are very tender, about 20–25 minutes. Mix salt, nonfat dry milk, cornstarch. Add cold water gradually and mix well. When potatoes are tender, pour this mixture into potatoes and mix well. Sprinkle Molly McButter on top and stir in. Beat with hand mixer until only tiny pieces of potato and onion remain. If too thick, stir in more water. Add pepper (1/4 to 1/2 tsp.) and parsley flakes, if desired, and serve hot. Reheat in microwave, or add water and stir constantly over medium heat. Yields 4 (1-cup) servings. (If made with 3 Tbs. cornstarch, add 7 calories and 7 grams carbohydrate.)

Nutrients per serving:		Exchanges:	
Calories	225	Bread	2
Fat	—	Milk	1
Cholesterol	—		
Carbohydrate	43g		
Sodium	546mg		

Refrigerate soups and stews to congeal fat, then lift off fat and discard it.

Use skim or lowfat milk in place of cream or whole milk to reduce calories, fat, and cholesterol in cream-based soup.

Vegetables

Salt by any other name:

Sodium nitrate
Sodium bicarbonate (baking soda)
Monosodium glutamate
Sodium benzoate (a preservative, usually 1/10th of 1% used)
Sodium phosphate

Heart patients who must watch salt intake should read labels for these ingredients. They should limit sodium to 400 mg. per serving of one food or 800 mg. per serving of a one-dish meal.

ASPARAGUS CASSEROLE

- 2 cans (10½-oz. size) tender asparagus
- 1 cup skim milk
- 3 Tbs. Fleischmann's Margarine
- 3 Tbs. flour
- 1 egg, hard-boiled, thinly sliced
- 12 Saltine crackers, crumbled
- 1 cup cheddar cheese, grated
- Pepper and paprika

Drain liquid from asparagus and combine with milk. Melt margarine; add flour to make cream sauce. Make 2 layers as follows: asparagus, sliced egg, crumbled crackers, cream sauce, and cheese. Sprinkle pepper and paprika on top and bake at 325 degrees about 30 minutes until casserole bubbles. Serve in 1/2-cup portions. Serves 4.

Nutrients per serving:		Exchanges:	
Calories	308	Bread	1
Fat	20g	Meat	2
Cholesterol	33mg	Vegetable	1
Carbohydrate	19g	Fat	2
Sodium	332mg		

PEAS AND ASPARAGUS CASSEROLE

1 can asparagus, drained
1 (15-oz.) can English peas, drained (Del Monte No Salt)
1 can cream of mushroom soup (Campbell's Special Request)
1 cup skim milk
1½ cups light cheddar process cheese, grated
1/2 cup cracker crumbs (without salt)

Place asparagus, then peas, in buttered baking dish. Mix soup, milk, and cheese. Pour over vegetables; sprinkle with cracker crumbs. Bake at 350 degrees for 30 minutes. Serve in 1/2-cup portions. Serves 8.

Nutrients per servings:	
Calories	112
Fat	4g
Cholesterol	5mg
Carbohydrate	16g
Sodium	373mg

Exchanges:	
Bread	1/2
Vegetable	1½
Fat	1

BAKED BEANS

1/2 medium onion, diced
1 diced bell pepper (optional)
2 Tbs. brown SugarTwin
1 Tbs. mustard seed
1 cup catsup (low-sodium)
1/2 tsp. garlic powder
1 Tbs. vinegar
1/4 can water
2 (15-oz.) cans pork and beans
1 strip bacon

Brown onion and peppers. Add other ingredients except beans and bacon. Simmer a few minutes. Pour over beans. Top with strips of bacon. Bake 1 hour at 350 degrees. Serve in 1/2-cup portions. Serves 8. (From Eva Dix.)

Nutrients per serving:	
Calories	161
Fat	1g
Cholesterol	.9mg
Carbohydrate	41g
Sodium	97mg

Exchanges:	
Bread	2
Vegetables	2

SWISSED GREEN BEANS

2 Tbs. margarine
1/4 lb. fresh mushrooms, sliced
1/2 cup chopped onion (1 small)
2 Tbs. flour
1/4 tsp. salt
1/4 tsp. pepper (optional)
1/3 cup lean sour cream
1/4 cup skim milk
2 (303 size) cans whole green beans
4 slices Borden's Lite Line process Swiss cheese
1/4 cup fine dry breadcrumbs

Melt 2 Tbs. margarine in frying pan. Add mushrooms and onion and sauté for 5 minutes. Mix in flour, salt, and pepper. Stir in sour cream and milk and heat through, but don't let it boil. Mix in well-drained green beans and cheese. Put in greased 2-qt. Corningware casserole. Top with breadcrumbs.

Bake at 350 degrees for 20 minutes or cook on high in microwave until everything is hot. Makes 8 servings of approximately 1/2 cup.

Nutrients per serving:	
Calories	117
Fat	5g
Cholesterol	8mg
Carbohydrate	7g
Sodium	417mg

Exchanges:	
Meat	1/2
Vegetable	1
Fat	1/2

Dark green and yellow vegetables have more vitamin A.

Don't put butter or margarine on vegetables before serving. Family members can add some at the table if they wish.

ORIENTAL GREEN BEANS

2 (10-oz.) pkg. frozen French-style green beans
1 can water chestnuts, sliced
2 (4-oz.) cans mushrooms or 6 large fresh mushrooms
1 (20-oz.) can bean sprouts
1 can low-sodium cream of mushroom soup
1 (3-oz.) can, or 1 pkg. French fried onion rings

Cook beans in 1 cup of boiling water. Put 1/2 of beans on bottom and cover with layers of 1/2 of everything else except onion rings. Repeat. Add onion rings if frozen. Bake 25 minutes at 325. Add onions if canned and bake 5 minutes more. Serves 8. Food values include two onion rings.

Nutrients per serving:		Exchanges:	
Calories	146	Vegetable	2
Fat	3g	Fat	1/2
Cholesterol	1.5mg		
Carbohydrate	9g		
Sodium	291mg with fresh mushrooms, 358mg if made with canned		

GREEN BEANS AND MUSHROOMS

2 cups frozen cut green beans
1 medium onion, chopped
3/4 to 1 cup fresh mushrooms
1 Tbs. margarine
2 slices grated lowfat American cheese (Borden's Lite Line)

Microwave beans on high (in dish with 1/4 tsp. salt and enough water to come halfway up to top of beans) for 7 minutes.

Meanwhile, sauté chopped onion and mushrooms in margarine until onion begins to turn transparent. Drain beans and put half on bottom of dish. Add onions and mushrooms; cover with remaining beans. Sprinkle grated cheese on top. Microwave on high 4–6 minutes more. Serves 4.

Nutrients per serving:		Exchanges:	
Calories	68	Vegetable	1
Fat	3.5g	Fat	1
Cholesterol	3mg		
Carbohydrate	5g		
Sodium	71mg		

Reducing the amount of salt you eat will reduce the amount of water your body holds and reduce your weight as well.

BROCCOLI CASSEROLE

1 (10-oz.) pkg. chopped broccoli
1 can cream of mushroom soup, low-sodium
1/2 cup sharp cheese, shredded
1/4 cup skim milk
1/4 cup light mayonnaise
1 egg, beaten
1/4 cup breadcrumbs
Parmesan cheese

Cook broccoli and drain. Add no salt. Put in bottom of casserole dish. Combine soup and cheese, then milk, mayonnaise and egg. Pour over broccoli. Put breadcrumbs on top. Sprinkle with Parmesan cheese. Bake at 350 degrees for 35 minutes. Serves 3 to 4.

Nutrients per serving:		Exchanges:	
Calories	161	Bread	1
Fat	7g	Meat	1
Cholesterol	75mg	Fat	1/2
Carbohydrate	17g		
Sodium	47mg		

CAROLYN'S BROCCOLI CASSEROLE

1 (10-oz.) pkg. frozen chopped broccoli
1 egg
1 cup nonfat yogurt (Dannon)
3/4 cup lowfat cottage cheese
1/2 cup Bisquick
1 tomato thinly sliced (optional)
2 Tbs. grated Parmesan cheese

Arrange broccoli (thaw enough to spread) on bottom of greased casserole, large glass pie pan, or Corningware dish. Beat egg and stir in yogurt and cottage cheese. Blend in Bisquick. Pour mixture over broccoli. Spread tomato slices on top and sprinkle Parmesan cheese over all. Bake at 350 degrees for 30 minutes or until firm on top. Serves 6.

Nutrients per serving:		Exchanges:	
Calories	124	Bread	1
Fat	3.5g	Fat	1
Cholesterol	47mg		
Carbohydrate	13.5g		
Sodium	324mg		

A medium-sized stalk of broccoli has 100% recommended daily allowance of Vitamin C, 40% of the RDA for Vitamin A, and is very low in calories.

BROCCOLI/CAULIFLOWER DISH

- 4 cups cauliflower buds
- 2 cups broccoli, diced
- 1/4 cup shredded cheddar cheese, sharp

Boil cauliflower and broccoli together in large pan until tender; drain. Place in large bowl. Sprinkle cheese over top while vegetables are still hot. Serves 6.

Nutrients per serving:	
Calories	45
Fat	1g
Cholesterol	3mg
Carbohydrate	6g
Sodium	71mg

Exchanges:	
Vegetable	1

PIZZA PLANT

- 1 large eggplant (about $1^1/_4$ lb. or 3 cups)
- 1/2 lb. ground beef (optional)
- 1 cup sliced mushrooms (optional)
- 1/2 cup chopped onion
- 4 cans (8-oz.) Hunt's Tomato Sauce (no salt added)
- 2 tsp. oregano
- 1 tsp. basil
- 1/2 tsp. garlic powder
- 1/4 tsp. pepper if desired
- 1/2 cup Parmesan cheese
- 6 oz. part-skim mozzarella cheese, coarsely grated

Slice eggplant in 1/4-inch-thick slices (discard ends) and steam (or simmer) 3 minutes until fork tender. (Or place in covered microwave dish with water $1^1/_2$ inches deep and microwave on high for $1^1/_2$ minutes.) Brown ground beef, mushrooms, and onion. Drain in a colander. If not using beef, sauté onion and mushrooms in a nonstick pan (if necessary add a few tablespoons of water to prevent burning). Add tomato sauce, oregano, basil, garlic powder, and pepper and simmer a few minutes. Spread Parmesan cheese on wax paper or plate. Coat both sides of eggplant slices with cheese and put half of them into 8 x 11 or 9 x 12 baking dish. Pour half of the meat sauce over the eggplant and sprinkle half of the grated mozzarella cheese on top. Repeat the process.

Bake at 350 for about 20 minutes or until mozzarella cheese is melted and lightly browned. Serves 8.

Nutrients per serving:		With Beef
Calories	140	217
Fat	6g	11g
Cholesterol	16mg	41mg
Carbohydrate	10g	12g
Sodium	321mg	430mg

Exchanges:		With Beef
Bread	1/2	1/2
Meat		1
Vegetable	1	1
Fat	1	1

BROCCOLI/SQUASH CASSEROLE

1 cup (2) yellow squash, diced
2 cups (1 lb.) broccoli, diced
Dash salt substitute
Molly McButter, to taste

Place diced squash and broccoli in large saucepan. Barely cover with water; add dash of salt substitute, and boil until tender. Drain. Serves 6. Let each person season with Molly McButter according to taste.

Nutrients per serving:	
Calories	21
Fat	—
Cholesterol	—
Carbohydrate	4g
Sodium	6mg

Exchanges:	
Vegetable	1

GARLIC GRITS

3 cups boiling water
1/2 tsp. salt
3/4 cup quick cooking grits, cooked as directed on box

Boil together for 10 minutes. Remove from heat.

Add:

1 beaten egg
1 beaten egg white
4 Tbs. Fleischmann's Margarine
8 oz. Borden's Lite Line Sharp Cheddar Cheese, grated
1 tsp. garlic powder
Dash of Tabasco

Mix together. Place in a 9 x 9-inch pan. Cook at 350 degrees for 30 to 35 minutes. Serves 10 in 1/2-cup portions.

Nutrients per serving:		Exchanges:	
Calories	66	Bread	1/2
Fat	9g	Fat	2
Cholesterol	43mg		
Carbohydrate	9g		
Sodium	312mg		

For variation include soft and crunchy foods in the same meal.

MUSHROOM FLORENTINA

1 (10-oz.) pkg. frozen chopped spinach
3 large fresh mushrooms, sliced or 4-oz. can of pieces
1 Tbs. melted margarine
1/2 tsp. salt
1 medium onion, chopped
2 slices Borden's Lite Line Process Sharp Cheddar Cheese
Garlic powder

Thaw spinach slightly in microwave (3 minutes on high in unopened package). Sauté mushrooms until brown in 1 Tbs. melted margarine. Mix spinach and salt, and place in 8-inch square casserole dish. Add chopped onion and sprinkle with half of the cheese. Add mushrooms and sprinkle those with garlic powder. Add rest of cheese. Bake 20 minutes at 350 or until cheese is melted and slightly browned. Serves 4.

Nutrients per serving:		Exchanges:	
Calories	63	Vegetable	1
Fat	3.5g	Fat	1
Cholesterol	3mg		
Carbohydrate	5g		
Sodium	71mg		

SCALLOPED POTATOES AND ONIONS

1 medium onion, thinly sliced and separated into rings
5 medium potatoes, thinly sliced
1/2 tsp. salt
1/4 tsp. pepper if desired
1/2 tsp. Adams imitation butter flavor
2 cups skim milk

Cut onion slices in half. Place layer of potatoes and layer of onion in small casserole dish, separating onion into half-rings as you spread it. Sprinkle part of the salt and pepper over this layer. Repeat until vegetables and seasonings are used up.

Mix butter flavor with milk and pour over potatoes. Bake in oven for 1 hour and 15 minutes at 400 degrees, or cook 15–20 minutes on high in the microwave and place a large plate under casserole to collect boiled-over liquid. Rotate dish in microwave 180 degrees when potatoes are half-done. (Oven baking soaks up more liquid than the microwave method.) Yields 10 (1/2-cup) servings.

Nutrients per serving:		Exchanges:	
Calories	81	Bread	1
Fat	—	Milk	1/2
Cholesterol	1mg		
Carbohydrate	17g		
Sodium	106mg		

Use garlic powder. Garlic salt has too much sodium!

CHEESE POTATOES

- 1 lb. frozen hash brown potatoes
- 1/2 cup chopped onions
- 1/2 can cream of chicken or mushroom soup (low-sodium)
- 1/2 cup light sour cream
- 2 Tbs. unsalted margarine
- 2 oz. grated sharp cheese

Mix and cook in a microwave oven for 20–24 minutes, rotating and stirring at 8 minutes and 16 minutes, until tender and cheese has melted.

If baked in regular oven, bake at 350 degrees for 50 to 60 minutes. If using shredded hash brown patties, first defrost on low in microwave for 7 minutes.

Note: This can be cooked in a crock pot for company dinner, but it takes about 4 hours. Yields 10 (1/3-cup) servings.

Nutrients per serving:		Exchanges:	
Calories	176	Bread	1
Fat	11g	Vegetable	1
Cholesterol	12mg	Fat	2
Carbohydrate	17g		
Sodium	132mg		

MUGWUMPS

4 medium to small potatoes
4 medium to large carrots
4 slices bacon
1 large onion

Peel and cut up potatoes and carrots. Add to boiling water. Use enough water to cover. Cook until soft enough to mash. While they cook, chop onion and cut slices of bacon into 1/2-inch squares. Fry bacon in frying pan until half done, then add the onion and cook both until the bacon is crisp and the onion is transparent.

Drain onion and bacon on paper towels or in a colander. If you wish to save bacon grease for other cooking, place colander over a bowl to collect drippings. Mash the potatoes and carrots. If the carrots are not quite done, this makes an interesting texture. Add the drained bacon and onion bits and mix well. Makes 6 servings of 1/3 cup each. You may wish to allow larger portions for the rest of the family.

Nutrients per serving:		Exchanges:	
Calories	132	Bread	1
Fat	2g	Vegetable	2
Cholesterol	4mg	Fat	1/2
Carbohydrate	23g		
Sodium	89mg		

Use lowfat yogurt instead of sour cream on baked potatoes.

RICE CASSEROLE

4 green onions, chopped
1/2 cup mushrooms, sliced
4 Tbs. (1/2 stick) margarine
1 tsp. oregano
1 cup rice, uncooked
2 cups hot beef broth (or 2 cups boiling water and 2 tsp. instant bouillon with no added salt)
2/3 cup water

Sauté first 4 ingredients together; add cup of rice and stir until rice is coated with melted margarine. Add beef broth and water. Bake 1 hour at 400 degrees. Serves 6. If desired, can add 1/2 cup more mushrooms for about 2 calories more per serving.

Nutrients per serving:		Exchanges:	
Calories	120	Bread	1½
Fat	7g	Vegetable	1
Cholesterol	21mg	Fat	1½
Carbohydrate	25g		
Sodium	340mg		

SPIRAL VEGGIE CASSEROLE

- 2 cups corkscrew vegetable-flavored rotini (Rainbow Rotini)
- 3 medium carrots, quartered and cut in bite-size pieces
- 4 cups boiling water
- 2 medium onions, chopped
- 1 Tbs. bacon drippings or margarine
- 2 cans (8-oz.) Hunt's No Salt Added Tomato Sauce
- 1/4 tsp. garlic powder
- 1 cup frozen corn
- 1/4 tsp. pepper to taste
- 1 Tbs. imitation bacon bits

Cook rotini and carrots in boiling water about 10 minutes or until rotini is soft and carrots are crisp-tender. Fry onion in bacon drippings until lightly browned. Drain rotini and carrots and add to onion. Add tomato sauce, garlic powder, corn, pepper, and bacon bits. Cook until heated through and carrots are tender. Makes 5 servings.

Nutrients per serving:		Exchanges:	
Calories	166	Bread	1
Fat	4g	Vegetable	2
Cholesterol	4mg	Fat	1
Carbohydrate	23g		
Sodium	109mg		

1/2 cup pasta has only 105 calories and very little sodium.

VEGETABLE NOODLE MEDLEY

8 oz. fine noodles
3/4 cup sliced carrots
2 1/2 cups sliced fresh mushrooms
1 cup chopped green pepper
1/2 cup sliced green onions, including stems
1 Tbs. margarine
1 can beef consommé
1/4 tsp. marjoram
1/2 tsp. garlic powder

Cook noodles and carrots in 6–8 cups boiling water with no salt added for 10 minutes. Brown mushrooms, green pepper, and onions in margarine. Drain noodles and carrots. Add to vegetables with consommé, marjoram, and garlic powder. Cook until heated through and carrots are crisp tender. Makes 7 (1-cup) servings.

Nutrients per serving:		Exchanges:	
Calories	162	Breads	1 1/2
Fat	2g	Vegetable	1
Cholesterol	2mg	Fat	1/2
Carbohydrate	28g		
Sodium	305mg		

SWEET POTATO CASSEROLE

3 cups cooked, mashed sweet potatoes
24 pkg. Equal
3 egg whites
2 Tbs. margarine, melted
1 cup skim milk
1/2 tsp. nutmeg
1/2 tsp. cinnamon
1 tsp. vanilla

Topping:
1/3 cup dry breadcrumbs
2 Tbs. brown sugar
1/4 cup chopped pecans
1 1/2 Tbs. melted margarine

Mix sweet potatoes, Equal, egg whites, melted margarine, milk, nutmeg, cinnamon, and vanilla. Spread in 8-inch square casserole dish and bake at 375 for 15 minutes. Mix topping and spread over top. Bake 15 minutes more at 375. In the microwave, cook 9 minutes on high the first time; rotate dish, add topping and cook 9 minutes more on high. Yields 8 (1/2-cup) servings.

Nutrients per serving:		Exchanges:	
Calories	220	Bread	2
Fat	7.7g	Fat	1 1/2
Cholesterol	.5mg		
Carbohydrate	33g		
Sodium	194mg		

Vary colors, shapes and sizes of vegetables for interesting meals.

2.

If a Heart Attack is Stalking You: Suggestions for Heart Patients

If the doctor has warned you that you're a candidate for a heart attack, don't resign yourself to doing without everything good. You will probably have to change your life a bit, but there are still plenty of good foods to eat.

Consult your doctor about your cholesterol and triglyceride levels. (Blood cholesterol levels under 200 are good. Levels between 200 and 239 mean you should try to reduce your cholesterol, and levels over 240 put you at risk for heart attacks.)

Things you can do to stay healthy include the following:

1. **Quit smoking, even if you've smoked for years.** Smoking lowers levels of high-density lipoprotein (HDL), which act to protect you against atherosclerosis (hardening of the arteries).(1) After you have gone a year without smoking, your cholesterol and HDL levels will probably return to normal.

2. **Lose weight.** Overweight people are more at risk for heart attacks. In 70 studies, 114 findings show a significant decrease in total cholesterol, low-density lipoproteins (LDL) and triglycerides, and an increase in high-density lipoproteins (HDL) with weight loss. Losing weight reduces your chance of having a heart attack.(2)

3. **Exercise.** Exercise helps you lose weight faster than just dieting and increases the amount of your high-density lipoprotein (HDL, a

heavy molecule combining fat with protein so it will dissolve in the blood), which helps protect you from heart attacks.(1) Ask your doctor what kind of exercise and how much you should do. Brisk walking for twenty to thirty minutes is something most people can do.

4. **Eat eggs and red meat in small amounts and less often.** One egg has 213–270 milligrams of cholesterol, and the recommended daily level for normal people is only 300 mg. Many dishes made with a small amount of red meat are very tasty.

5. **Cut the amount of fat you eat to a bare minimum.** Watch out for fat you can see on meat (especially beef and pork) and hidden fats in cream soup, desserts made with whipped cream, creamy salad dressings, gravy and fried foods. Don't just watch out for it, dodge it whenever you can.

6. **Avoid saturated fats as much as possible.** Usually solid at room temperature, animal fats found in eggs, meat (especially red meats and pork), whole milk, hard cheeses, butter, and ice cream are saturated fat. People who eat a lot of these foods are more likely to have heart attacks than those who don't.

Drink skim milk instead. If you prefer whole milk (3.5% fat), try working your way down to milk with lower fat by mixing it with skim milk to get used to the taste. Then gradually work down to mostly skim milk or at least milk with only ½–1% fat.

Use margarines made with oil and lowfat cheeses. Watch out for a few plant foods with saturated fats, such as avocado and coconut oil, often found in coffee creamers.

7. **Use polyunsaturated fats.** These are usually liquid at room temperature and are found mostly in plant foods, such as safflower oil, corn oil, sunflower oil, and margarines made with them. If you fry foods, use a nonfat spray, such as Pam, a small amount of the oils mentioned above, or margarine made with those oils. You can brown meat without adding extra fat if you turn it often.

8. **Mix monounsaturated fats such as olive oil with polyunsaturated oils for cooking and salads.** Monounsaturated oils tend to lower the levels of total cholesterol and the LDL (low-density lipoprotein, which is bad for you) while leaving the HDL level alone.

9. **Eat fish with Omega-3 fatty acid (eicosapentaenoic acid).** This is the monounsaturated fatty acid that tends to thin out the blood and make it less likely to form clots to clog arteries. Eskimos, who have a very low level of coronary heart disease, eat a lot of bonito, herring, mackerel, salmon, and whitefish, which lowers their chances of

heart attacks. Other sources of Omega-3 fatty acid are sea trout, bass, bluefish, and halibut.(1)

10. **Cut way down on salt.** Choose side dish recipes with less than 400 milligrams (mg) of sodium or main dish casseroles under 800 mg sodium.

Salt encourages high blood pressure, which can lead to a heart attack. Smoked ham and bacon are not only high in salt, but they have been shown to cause formation of nitrosamines, which tend to cause cancer. Instead of salt, try out different spices in your food for a change of pace.

11. **Cut down on stress.** Surely your job can be done well without wearing you to a frazzle. Don't try to accomplish everything at once. Plan time to relax and do things you enjoy for a change of pace. Make a "Joy List" of activities you like to do that take fifteen minutes, an hour, half a day, or a whole day and reward yourself by working them into your schedule (as suggested by a Dallas time management expert, Ann McGee-Cooper).

A job change may help you enjoy life more and live longer. If it's not practical to change jobs, try relaxation exercises to relieve stress.

12. **Eat oat bran.** Oat bran has been shown to reduce cholesterol levels.(1) Oatmeal with oat bran tastes the same, and works just as well in recipes calling for oatmeal.

13. **If necessary, take drugs to reduce cholesterol under a doctor's supervision.** Some people inherit tendencies to have high cholesterol and are in danger of heart attacks at an early age if drastic measures are not taken. If your cholesterol level remains abnormally high, you need to follow a strict program of diet, exercise, and drugs under a doctor's supervision to avoid heart attacks.

REFERENCES

1. Kenneth H. Cooper, M.D., *Controlling Cholesterol* (New York: Bantam Books, 1988), 86, 216, 258, 278, 281.

2. Anne M. Dattilo and Kris-Etherton, P. M., "Effects of Weight Reduction on Blood Lipids and Lipoproteins: A Meta Analysis" *American Journal of Clinical Nutrition* 56, no. 2 (August 1992): 320–326.

3.

Suggestions for Diabetics

The doctor has told you that you have diabetes — what now? Listen to his instructions. An appointment with a dietitian should provide you with a recommended diet and answer your basic questions.

Since your pancreas may not produce enough insulin to turn all the sugar you want to eat into energy, you need to follow the diet and take prescribed medication for as long as the doctor tells you to.

If you control your blood sugar by watching your diet and taking insulin or a pancreas-boosting medicine (if needed), you should live a long, healthy life. However, you need to be aware of the dangers if you don't take care of yourself.

Controlling your blood sugar keeps you healthy. A blood-monitoring machine, which health insurance often pays for, will show your blood sugar count. When it gets too high, you probably ate foods containing too much sugar. If you watch your blood sugar count, avoid eating foods high in sugar, take the correct amount of medication, and eat well-balanced meals on a regular schedule, you can keep your body on an even keel and avoid getting the shakes, insulin shock, or diabetic coma. When your body doesn't have enough sugar for the brain to work properly, insulin shock can happen. While not common, diabetic coma results if you accumulate too much sugar in the blood and have not taken enough insulin at the proper time. The right amount of insulin must be balanced with proper meals and regular exercise.

What you can eat. Does this mean you can never eat sweets again? An occasional (that's once a month, not once a day) serving (small, not hippo-sized) shouldn't hurt — if you're eating a balanced diet and taking insulin if prescribed.

However, you may not feel sure about eating some things. It's hard to avoid sugar entirely, but look on the labels of foods to see which include sugar, honey, or corn syrup. If it is the second, third, or fourth ingredient listed — which means there is more of only one, two or three ingredients besides sugar — avoid that food.

Don't make the mistake of thinking honey or corn syrup are okay because they aren't refined sugar. Table sugar is made up of glucose and fructose. Honey, corn syrup, and light molasses hold just as much glucose or fructose as table sugar. Fructose (also called fruit sugar) is sometimes used to keep calories low because it is sweeter and manufacturers can use less to make a food taste good. However, it is still sugar.

Carbohydrates come in two basic forms: starches and sugars. The starches, such as bread and starchy vegetables like potatoes, are composed of large molecules and must be broken down into the simpler molecules (the sugars) in order to be digested, which takes longer.

The sugars come in small molecules, are very concentrated sources of energy, and can be quickly digested. However, you don't produce enough insulin for your body to use up a large amount of sugar. When you eat too much sugar, it will pile up in your blood. If not controlled, this overload of sugar in the blood may eventually lead to eye problems, high blood pressure, kidney problems, and poor circulation.

The carbohydrates you eat should be mostly starches, and you should only eat as many servings per meal as allowed on your prescribed diet. These digest slowly and give off small amounts of sugar that the body can use up for energy right away. There should not be more sugar in your blood than you can use for energy in a short time.

The sweets you eat should be raw or unsweetened fruit because that also takes longer to digest and gives off only small amounts of sugar at a time to your blood. The concentrated sugar in candy, cake, or cookies will be digested quickly to deliver an overload of sugar to your blood, which is why you should avoid them.

Most diets prescribed for diabetics allow you to eat several servings of fruit per day. This helps satisfy your sweet tooth without endangering your health. Sugar-free Jell-O brand gelatin and puddings usually taste good and can be used as a base for desserts and salads. Use skim milk instead of whole to keep the fat content low.

Recipes for delicious desserts in this book use fruit, artificial sweeteners, and sometimes a teaspoon of sugar per serving (an amount dieticians have said will not overload your body if you eat only one serving of the recommended size in one day). While desserts can be made with only artificial sweeteners, many do not taste good enough to be satisfying.

Staying healthy. If you control your blood sugar by checking blood sugar level, taking the right amount of insulin, and eating the proper diet at regular mealtimes, you can expect to live a long, healthy life. And with this book, you can enjoy eating too.

QUICK REFERENCE LIST FOR DIABETICS

Note: For exchange list of recommended serving sizes, see Appendix B.

Things to stay away from:

Sugar	Pie	Sugared Cereals
Candy	Cake	Beer (1 okay occasionally)
Honey	Pastries	Wine (1 okay occasionally)
Jam, Jelly, Marmalade	Soft Drinks	Alcoholic Beverages (1 okay occasionally)
Syrups, Molasses	Regular Gum	

Freebies (Have all you want):

Diet Soft Drinks, sugar-free, caffeine-free	Lemons
Coffee, Tea, sugar-free, caffeine-free	Sugar-free Gelatin
Clear Broth, Bouillon (fat-free)	Unsweetened Pickles

Near Freebies:

Popcorn	Sugar-free Gelatin, Puddings
Sugar-free Gum	Four Square Candy (see recipe)
Sugar-free Popsicle	Sugarless Candy (Velements taste like Lifesavers)
Nutrasweet Ice Cream Bar	
Diet Colas (no more than four per day)	

4.

How Diet, Life-style, and Heredity Affect Your Weight

Do you feel as if you were destined to be wider than a whale? Can you blame it on your genes? It's true that heredity determines where your body builds up fatty deposits. Heredity also influences metabolism, the rate at which your body burns calories. So does your childhood family's life-style.

If your family ate fat-rich foods, used sweets to reward children, and didn't get much exercise, you are likely to continue the same life-style, which encourages weight gain.

You just enjoy eating. Like the authors of this book and many others, you enjoy eating. Seeing and tasting good food makes you want to eat more. I find I can resist rich foods more easily if I don't see them. If I take "just one bite," I often give in and eat more. Then I'm tempted to blow my diet for the rest of the day.

Does age make a difference? As you get older, you tend to add pounds, even though you eat the same amount of food. This may be partly due to becoming less active. However, a decreasing rate of metabolism means your body needs less food even though your appetite remains the same. It hit me at thirty, when I stopped carrying two-year-old twins and had to start watching my weight.

When my daughters were six, I took up jogging to keep from gaining weight. Now that I'm older, I have to watch my diet more carefully. You may have to eat less, exercise more, or do both to keep your weight where you want it.

Have you been feeding a gazelle body elephant fare? Try listing what you eat during a typical day on a piece of paper. Be honest. No one but you will see this. Figure out how many servings of each food group you usually eat, estimate the calories for each according to the following chart, and write in the amounts on the page. (Check serving sizes in Appendix B.)

Compare the total with the calorie allowance for the weight recommended for your height. If you are eating more, you have an active metabolism — or you are probably gaining weight.

Calories per serving	*Your calories*
Milk Group — 90 calories for skim milk, 150 for whole milk.	
Bread Group (also pasta, potatoes, cereal) — 80 calories per serving.	
Fruits — 60 calories per serving.	
Vegetables — 25 calories per serving.	
Meats — 165 calories per 3-oz. serving of lean meat or fish, 300–350 per 3-oz. serving of high-fat meat (dinner meat servings are usually 3–4 oz.)	
Fat — 50 calories per serving (1 pat butter, margarine, 1/2 Tbs. dressing).	
Your total	________

New York wasn't built in a week, and neither were you. Those pounds didn't suddenly plaster themselves on your body. Examine your life-style for things that contributed to your weight gain.

1. If you let the pounds pile up without noticing until your clothes threaten to sue for wearer brutality, weigh daily.

2. Next time you eat between meals, ask yourself if you're really hungry or just want to eat something good. If you eat because you're bored, start a new hobby. (Lion taming, maybe?)

3. If you eat to keep food from being wasted, give leftovers to the dog. Try to prepare less next time. Even dogs get fat.

4. If you eat too much high-calorie food, substitute lower calorie items. You can have small amounts of your favorite dishes on special occasions. (Watching "Monday Night Football" is *not* a special occasion.)

5. Watch out for chips and crackers you hardly notice eating

while watching television. Don't eat anything, or try vegetables with a low calorie dip or popcorn without butter.

6. If you eat extra calories without realizing it — like the visible fat on meat, butter on vegetables, high-calorie salad dressing — become more aware of fat and sugar content when you shop. Sugar concentrates a lot of calories into a few bites. Labels are required to list ingredients in order of their proportion in the food. If the second ingredient is sugar, the food has more sugar than anything else except the first ingredient.

7. Watch out for foods with a high-calorie count:

Dairy Queen's large chocolate malt . . . 1,020 calories
(try their small cone with 140 calories)

McDonald's Quarter Pounder with cheese . . . 510 calories
(eat their Chicken Fajitas with 185 calories)

Arby's Superstuffed Deluxe Baked Potato . . . 648 calories
(choose their Junior Roast Beef with 220 calories)

Chocolate cake . . . 350 or more
(try our Carrot Cake with 176 calories)

Even if you don't need to avoid sweets entirely, remember that on a 1,200 calorie diet, a piece of chocolate cake has enough calories for a whole breakfast or lunch. So save cake for special occasions.

8. Maybe you eat as usual, but get less exercise than before. If so, eat less and exercise more. (Play tiddly-winks or dodge-ball with manhole covers.) Try something you enjoy.

9. If you find yourself using food to reward yourself for working hard, try a movie, a new book, or record instead.

10. While carbohydrates (starches and especially sugars) will comfort you when you feel depressed, watch out for a tendency to overeat when you use food to make you feel better. According to Judith J. Wurtman, who has a doctorate in nutritional biochemistry, eating carbohydrate-rich foods helps tryptophan (an amino acid in protein) to reach the brain, which increases the amount of a natural tranquilizer called serotonin in the brain and makes you feel relaxed.(1) (2)

Quickly digested, lowfat carbohydrates, such as fruit juice, in small amounts, help you feel relaxed with less danger of gaining weight. This helps ease temporary stress.

People who react to unhappiness by continually overeating should consider counseling as a first step in controlling weight.

If some things listed above sound familiar, it will be easy to spot your problem areas. Know your weaknesses where food is concerned, then find ways around them.

If you've tried dieting. After a diet were you tempted to eat the same way you did before? If you were, have you gained all those pounds back and maybe an unwanted bonus of a few more? Are the clothes you saved until you got thin still too small? Could the cleaners have shrunk them?

Perhaps you lost for a while, then got caught up in the yo-yo syndrome, a pattern of crash dieting and regaining.

Kelly Brownell, Ph.D., observed a group of Philadelphia women having a hard time losing weight. He put laboratory animals through two cycles of unlimited food followed by dieting.

During the second cycle the animals became fat sooner and took longer to lose the weight. Women who had dieted before had the same pattern of weight regain after dieting.(3) (4) Studies show people tend to maintain a lower rate of metabolism (the rate the body uses calories) for five to eight weeks after being on a severe low-calorie diet, which may cause the tendency to regain lost pounds.(4) (5)

Feel like you're stuck on overweight? The set-point theory comes from studies done on people and animals who were "starved" and "stuffed" for periods before being allowed to eat at their own rate. The subjects tended to return to a certain weight and stay close to it.

At the end of a six-month study of carefully controlled dieting, the volunteers' compulsions to eat and their irritability didn't stop until the amount of fat in their bodies and their weight returned to what it was before. That could explain why you feel hungry even when you eat the right amount of calories for your proper weight.

Protein amounts were carefully figured for the starvation diet, but it took nine months after weight returned to normal for the volunteers' muscle tissue to be restored. More recent studies indicate the body tends to retain the same proportion of fat to lean tissue when you lose weight and that loss of some lean tissue is not harmful.(7) However, it's important to eat enough protein while on a diet.

According to Dr. William Bennett and Joel Gurin in *The Dieter's Dilemma,* the brain makes you hungry. They claim that your body decides for itself the ratio of bone, muscle, and fat it needs and will fight to keep it that way. The authors say that the only safe way to lower the set-point (the weight at which your body naturally tends to stay) is through physical activity. The trick is to exercise vigorously long enough to burn more calories than you eat and use up fat instead of muscle tissue.(6)

To attain a "set-point-balance," choose the right combination of food and activities to get your weight at a desirable level and maintain that weight. If you spend a lot of time sitting, don't eat like Henry the hippo. Even he gets up and moves around sometimes.

You may find that your body tends to maintain a set-point at a higher weight than you like. In order to keep your weight where you want it, you will have to watch your diet and exercise regularly. You may have to adjust to eating less food than the amount that makes you feel full or eat more of the filling, high-fiber foods.

Those awful bulges. Spot-reducing exercises don't help much. Eat enough protein and exercise vigorously to work that stubborn fat loose. Work into the exercises gradually so you won't be sore. Men tend to lose abdominal fat, and women tend to lose hip fat. Fatty tissue inside may be reduced by exercise before the waist-to-hip ratio changes; for women it often takes a loss of fifteen pounds.

Vigorous exercise may increase your appetite, but it also raises your metabolism rate during the time you exercise and for a short time after, so that you actually burn more calories.(6)

In time your appetite will adjust somewhat, even though you may still want to eat more of the fattening foods we all like. But, if you maintain your set-point-balance by developing habits of eating and exercising that will keep your weight stable, you'll be a winner.

Be the master of your fate. Design a healthy new life-style. Practice until it becomes a habit.

REFERENCES

1. Judith Wurtman, Ph.D., *Managing Your Mind and Mood Through Food* (New York: Rawson Associates, 1986), 18–23, 229–235.

2. Philippa Lyons, M., B.S., and A. Stewart Truswell, M.D., "Serotonin Precursor Influenced by Type of Carbohydrate Meal in Healthy Adults," *The American Journal of Clinical Nutrition* 47, no. 3 (March 1988): 433–438.

3. Kelly Brownell, Ph.D., "The Effects of Repeated Cycles of Weight Loss and Regain in Rats," *Physiol. Behav.* 38 (1986): 459–464.

4. G. L. Blackburn, G. T. Wilson, B.S. Kanders, et al., "Weight Cycling: The Experience of Human Dieters," *American Journal of Clinical Nutrition,* supplement to vol. 49, (May 1989): 1105–1109.

5. Diane L. Elliot, Linn Goldberg, Kerry S. Kuehl, and William M. Bennett, "Sustained Depression of the Resting Metabolic Rate after Massive Weight Loss," *American Journal of Clinical Nutrition* 49, no. 1 (January 1989): 93–96.

6. William Bennett, M.D., and Joel Gurin, *The Dieter's Dilemma* (New York: Basic Books, Inc., 1982), 11–23, 74–79, 92, 223–224, 251–255, 259–261.

7. Andrew M. Prentice, Susan A. Jebb, Gail R. Goldberg, William A. Coward, Peter R. Murgatroyd, Sally D. Poppitt, and Timothy J. Cole, "Effects of Weight Cycling on Body Composition," *American Journal of Clinical Nutrition,* supplement to vol. 56, no. 1 (July 1992): 209S–211S.

5.

If You're Serious About Losing Weight: Simple to Use Food Plans

Shedding strategy: To reduce your ankles, start with your mouth. Going on a diet is like writing a book. Wanting to be thinner and working at it now and then isn't enough. *Nothing happens unless you make a plan and stick to it until you succeed.*

If you've decided to become thinner and healthier, congratulations! With a few adjustments in your life-style, you can have an attractive, healthy body.

With the delicious recipes in this book, you can cut down on fat, sugar, and salt and still enjoy good food.

Diving in. Experts recommend seeing a doctor before you start, to be sure you have no mysterious disease (tapeworm from outer space, voodoo spell), any medical problem causing you to be overweight, or conditions that would be aggravated by dieting. *However, most weight gain is due to eating more calories than you need for your daily activities.*

Once you achieve a desirable weight, you want to maintain control. Learn to balance the calories you eat and your activity to reach a "set-point-balance" to keep your weight stable (see Chapter 4 for more explanation).

It's easy to add healthier ways of eating and exercise to your life-style. Cook the same healthful dishes for the whole family, but don't let on that it's good for them — or you'll have to eat it all while they head out for pizza. (We have a good pizza recipe too.) If you think you haven't time for exercise, remember that studies predict you'll live longer if you do it regularly.

For special dishes that take a little longer to prepare, make double and save half to reheat for another meal.

Don't just hobble your habits — transform them. Replace poor habits with good ones. Instead of dessert, eat raw fruit or drink coffee, spiced tea, or a diet cola. Stop nibbling while you watch television. Try painting, knitting, or making something nice for yourself.

Reinforce your resolutions. Use a wide fiber-tip pen to write your goals in large, bold letters on a piece of paper or an index card. Put it where you'll see it daily. For example: "I WILL NOT EAT BETWEEN MEALS" or "SLENDER BY SEPTEMBER." Tape a picture taken when you were thinner to the refrigerator. Look in the mirror as you wash your hands for a meal. Think how good you will look when you have slimmed down. Promise yourself something nice (and I don't mean a hot fudge sundae) after you stick to your plan for two weeks.

How many calories are right for you? Make it easy on yourself — and your body. Your brain needs 500 calories per day. Eating less than 1,000 calories per day may make you tired and hungry. Besides that, your disposition might be perfect for playing a villain in Goldilocks and the three you-know-whats.

With too few calories, you may not get enough vitamins, minerals, and protein. Like adding oil without enough gasoline to a car, adding vitamins without enough food won't help your body run well. If you feel you might not get enough vitamins, use a supplement providing 100% of the recommended daily allowance (R.D.A.). *Taking more than the R.D.A. can be harmful.*(1)

Besides being unhealthy, extremely strict diets are doomed to fail. "Super-low-calorie diets all have the same gimmick," said Dr. C. Wayne Callaway, director of the Center for Clinical Nutrition at George Washington University of Medicine. He explained that when you starve yourself, you lose water which will return when you eat normally.(2) Also, such diets force your body to burn muscle tissue for energy. As a natural protection against starvation, your body will restore lost fat before rebuilding muscles.(2) (3) Find the recommended weight for your height and frame size and calorie allowances on the following charts. If you eat 500 calories less daily, you should lose one to two pounds per week.

HEIGHT AND WEIGHT TABLES

Height (Men) (1″ heels)		Frame Small	Medium	Large
5	2	128–134	131–141	138–150
5	3	130–136	133–143	140–153
5	4	132–138	135–145	142–156
5	5	134–140	137–148	144–160
5	6	136–142	138–151	146–164
5	7	138–145	142–154	148–168
5	8	140–148	145–157	152–172
5	9	142–151	148–160	155–176
5	10	144–154	151–163	158–180
5	11	146–157	154–166	161–184
6	0	149–160	157–170	164–188
6	1	152–164	160–174	168–192
6	2	155–168	164–178	172–197
6	3	158–172	167–182	176–202
6	4	162–176	171–187	181–207

Height (Women) (1″ heels)		Frame Small	Medium	Large
4	10	102–111	108–121	118–131
4	11	103–113	111–123	120–134
5	0	104–115	113–126	122–137
5	1	106–118	115–129	125–140
5	2	108–121	118–132	128–143
5	3	111–124	121–135	131–147
5	4	114–127	124–138	134–151
5	5	117–130	127–141	137–155
5	6	120–133	130–144	140–158
5	7	123–136	133–147	143–163
5	8	126–139	136–150	146–167
5	9	129–142	139–153	148–170
5	10	132–145	142–156	152–173
5	11	135–148	145–158	155–176
6	0	136–151	148–162	158–179

Figures from Metropolitan Insurance Companies (1983)

CALORIE ALLOWANCES FOR NUDE BODY WEIGHTS

MEN				WOMEN			
Pounds	25 yrs.	45 yrs.	65 yrs.	Pounds	25 yrs.	45 yrs.	65 yrs.
132	2,422	2,295	1,913	88	1,488	1,403	1,200
143	2,550	2,380	1,998	99	1,615	1,530	1,275
154	2,720	2,550	2,168	110	1,743	1,658	1,360
165	2,890	2,720	2,295	121	1,870	1,743	1,488
176	3,018	2,848	2,380	128	1,955	1,870	1,530
187	3,145	2,975	2,465	132	1,998	1,913	1,573
198	3,249	3,071	2,525	143	2,125	1,998	1,700
209	3,366	3,198	2,609	154	2,210	2,083	1,743
				165	2,338	2,210	1,828

Figures adapted from Food, The Yearbook of Agriculture, 1959, *published by the United States Department of Agriculture in 1959.(4) (Figures for moderate activity have been reduced by 15% to reflect today's more sedentary life-style.)*

Why not try appetite controls? Appetite suppressants such as amphetamines and similar compounds are addicting. Studies show that animals and people return to the same appetite and weight after they stop taking the drugs. Both amphetamines and over-the-counter remedies containing Phenylpropanolamine have side effects. Interfering with digestion by stomach stapling or intestinal bypass surgery can cause medical complications.

Banish "fatty patty" and "big rig" from your mirror. Choose a food plan. Like me, you've probably tried the "Seafood Diet" (Anything I see, I eat), "Veggies Only" (Ugh!), and "Never Go Hungry Diet" (you won't get hungry, but you won't lose either.) Now lose weight with ours, which is simple, nutritionally balanced, and modeled after Meal Planning with Exchange Lists developed by committees of the American Diabetic Association, Inc., and Weight Watchers exchange lists.

The food plans have easy-to-remember food group servings. All you have to count is the number of servings of fruit, meat, fat, bread, vegetables, and milk products.

After you choose a food plan, check the amounts allowed for each exchange in Appendix B and note the few foods not allowed. Weigh or measure foods until you get used to the portion sizes.

Next, set a realistic goal and a time period. Losing one to two pounds per week seems slow, but doctors recommend that as a safe rate. That will be easier to maintain for a long period of time, and the pounds are less likely to return.

Usually a person's weight will vary a few pounds from day to day. Weigh yourself at the same time every day, wearing about the same amount of clothes. If you find it depressing to weigh every day, weigh weekly. (For maximum encouragement, do it nude before breakfast when weight is lowest.) If you gained several pounds, the shock should help you be super motivated that day. Pounds may drop fast when you first begin. After that, your weight may stay the same for several days or go up and down a pound or two before dropping again. Since individuals vary, you may need to adjust calorie amounts to reach your desired weight.

Shop like Sherlock Holmes. Study labels on food. Labels are required to list ingredients in the order of the percentage found in the food. If fat or sugar is one of the first four ingredients, choose another brand.

Heart patients should avoid foods high in fat or sodium such as pork, bacon, and ham (see Chapter 2). Diabetics should avoid foods high in sugar, corn syrup, and honey (see Chapter 3).

Plan ahead. Be sure to eat meals at regular times. I worked in a restaurant, and no matter how often I resolved not to eat forbidden goodies, if I didn't eat a good breakfast, pretty soon my resistance dwindled and I took "just a bite or two." And, of course, it seldom stops there. (Management suggested tasting the dessert of the day — could they have been conspiring against me?)

If coffee breaks at work occur over Danishes and doughnuts, bring your own low-calorie snack. (See our recipe for Cinnamon English Muffin Half.) It helps to have lowfat crackers at home. Graham crackers are only 25 calories per square and not that exciting to eat, so you won't do much damage. Watch out for your favorite high-calorie snack. Don't keep any around. Like Valentine's Day chocolates, they sneak up and pop in your mouth when you're not looking.

Stick-to-it-ive-ness slims. If you diet and lose several pounds, then hit a plateau, don't give up.

My friend Rosa is vivacious, with a pretty face and long, curly hair. Four years ago she was a shade past pleasingly plump. She would lick her lips, then shake her head at goodies before drinking diet powder "milkshakes." Later, she bubbled with enthusiasm and announced she was dieting under a doctor's care. Beginning each new diet with real determination, she would shell out money and follow each diet faithfully — for a while. Today she is two shades past pleasingly plump. But Mary, who had a lot more to lose than Rosa, ate a limited number of servings from each food group and soon lost enough for friends to notice.

Don't give up. It takes longer to lose those last few pounds, but once you're over the hump, you may drop several pounds. Losing will be harder if you quit dieting for a while before trying again.(5) (6) It helps you stick to a diet if you plan a special dinner (without calorie limits) once every two weeks. *STICKING TO THE DIET LONG ENOUGH AND EXERCISING REGULARLY PRODUCES RESULTS!*

Easy to Remember Food Plans with Measured Calories

The numbers in each column tell how many servings are allowed for each meal. Diabetics should eat only two bread units per meal unless doctors advise otherwise. For a well-balanced daily diet use Chapter 3 Menu Plans or include: A. Bread and cereals, 4–6 servings; B. Fruits and vegetables, 5–6 (include 1 citrus fruit and 1 dark green or yellow vegetable); C. Milk, 2 (3–4 for women); and D. Meat, fish, cheese, 6 oz. (meat servings are 1 oz.).

1,000 Calorie Food Plan

	Starch/Bread	Meats/Substitutes	Vegetables	Fruit	Milk	Fat
Bkfst.	1			1		(0)
Lunch	1	2	1*	1	1/2	
Supper	1	3 (lowfat types)	2*	1	1/2	

1,200 Calorie Food Plan

	Starch/Bread	Meats/Substitutes	Vegetables	Fruit	Milk	Fat
Bkfst.	1	1		1	1	1
Lunch	2	2	1*	2	1/2	
Supper	1	2 (lowfat types)	2*	1	1/2	

1,500 Calorie Food Plan

	Starch/Bread	Meats/Substitutes	Vegetables	Fruit	Milk	Fat
Bkfst.	1	1		1	1	2
Lunch	2	2	1*	2	1/2	1
Supper	2	3	2*	1	1/2	1

1,800 Calorie Food Plan

	Starch/Bread	Meats/Substitutes	Vegetables	Fruit	Milk	Fat
Bkfst.	1	1		1	1	1
Lunch	2	2	1	1	1/2	2
Supper	2	3	2*	2	1/2	2

2,000 Calorie Food Plan

	Starch/Bread	Meats/Substitutes	Vegetables	Fruit	Milk	Fat
Bkfst.	1	2		2	1	2
Lunch	2	2	1	2	1/2	1
Supper	2 + 1/2	4	2	1	1	2

2,300 Calorie Food Plan

	Starch/Bread	Meats/Substitutes	Vegetables	Fruit	Milk	Fat
Bkfst.	3	2		2	1	2
Lunch	3	2	1	2	1/2	3
Supper	4	4	2	1	1	2

2,500 Calorie Food Plan

	Starch/Bread	Meats/Substitutes	Vegetables	Fruit	Milk	Fat
Bkfst.	3	2		2	1	2
Lunch	3	2	1	2	1	3
Supper	4	4	2	2	1	2

2,900 Calorie Food Plan

	Starch/Bread	Meats/Substitutes	Vegetables	Fruit	Milk	Fat
Bkfst.	3 + 1/2	2		2	1	2
Lunch	4	3	1	2	1	3
Supper	4	4	2	2	1	2

* One vegetable should be a very low-calorie type, such as [2–3 (1-cup) servings per day for diabetics]: Raw cabbage, celery, Chinese cabbage, cu-

cumber, green onion, hot pepper, mushrooms, radishes, zucchini, lettuce, spinach, escarole, romaine.

These food plans are simple to follow. Write the number of servings for each group from the food plan you choose in the first food plan that follows. Photocopy the blank food plans to take with you to keep track of what you eat. Stay within the limits of the plan and you'll see a slimmer you in the mirror.

PLAN FOR A NEW YOU

Fill in number of servings from your chosen food plan.

	Starch/ Bread	Meats/Fish	Eggs, Cheese	Vegetables	Fruit	Milk	Fat
Bkfst.							
Lunch							
Supper							

KEEP TRACK OF WHAT YOU EAT: Mark down each serving you eat.

SUNDAY

	Starch/ Bread	Meats/Fish	Eggs, Cheese	Vegetables	Fruit	Milk	Fat
Bkfst.							
Lunch							
Supper							

MONDAY

	Starch/ Bread	Meats/Fish	Eggs, Cheese	Vegetables	Fruit	Milk	Fat
Bkfst.							
Lunch							
Supper							

TUESDAY

	Starch/ Bread	Meats/Fish	Eggs, Cheese	Vegetables	Fruit	Milk	Fat
Bkfst.							
Lunch							
Supper							

WEDNESDAY

	Starch/ Bread	Meats/Fish	Eggs, Cheese	Vegetables	Fruit	Milk	Fat
Bkfst.							
Lunch							
Supper							

THURSDAY

	Starch/ Bread	Meats/Fish	Eggs, Cheese	Vegetables	Fruit	Milk	Fat
Bkfst.							
Lunch							
Supper							

FRIDAY

	Starch/ Bread	Meats/Fish	Eggs, Cheese	Vegetables	Fruit	Milk	Fat
Bkfst.							
Lunch							
Supper							

SATURDAY

	Starch/ Bread	Meats/Fish	Eggs, Cheese	Vegetables	Fruit	Milk	Fat
Bkfst.							
Lunch							
Supper							

Remember the tortoise and the hare: slow progress is better!

You're wise to avoid fad diets. When you diet sensibly, the pounds stay off better. Many fad diets interfere with your metabolism (the process of creating energy from food). Protein needs six times as much water for digestion as carbohydrates. High-protein diets pull off fluid that returns when you stop that diet. (Every time I've tried that high-protein, low-carbohydrate diet, I gained five pounds back as soon as I stopped.) Staying on the high-protein, low-carbohydrate diet very long may induce ketosis (a concentration of ketones in your body). This can endanger your health. If you are still tempted to try any of the fad diets which promise fast results, remember:

1. *Many diets do not provide all the foods needed for good health.* You may take vitamins, but they can't work without food. Vitamins don't include the protein you need.

2. *A semi-starvation diet makes you feel tired and weak.* You wouldn't have the energy to go out with Tom Selleck or Madonna.

3. *Many fad diets are so monotonous* you're tempted to quit before losing the desired weight (maybe by the second meal).

4. *Fad diets are not designed with your preferences in mind.* Sauerkraut anyone?

5. *Your new eating pattern should include foods you like and should be similar to one you can use to keep your desired weight.* Don't like fish? This book offers many tasty alternatives.

6. *Some diets promote myths* such as "eating grapefruit burns off your fat" or "eating carbohydrates adds pounds." That makes as much sense as pounding your stomach flat with a wooden mallet.

7. *Some fad diets may kill you.* Since liquid protein diets have resulted in several deaths, the Department of Agriculture has ruled that those diets based on less than 500 calories must be supervised by a doctor.

Even carefully supervised patients have developed potentially life-threatening arrhythmias (the heartbeat irregularities blamed in liquid protein deaths) that were only discovered on a "sophisticated system of round-the-clock heart monitoring."(3)

How You Can Banish "Fatty Patty" and "Big Rig" Forever

Many diet and lose, only to regain lost weight. The secret is to change your life-style just enough to maintain your weight.

Balance the calories you eat and your activity. Don't return to the poor eating habits that helped you gain those unwanted pounds. Increase calories slowly after dieting. Your body will have a reduced rate of metabolism (it uses fewer calories to give you the same amount of energy) for a while after you stop dieting.(6) Avoid fats and high-calorie dishes. *In order to maintain your weight, you must balance your calorie intake and activity. When your weight creeps up, reduce your calories and exercise more.*

Exercise helps you banish fat. Moderately overweight young women who ate 1,800 calories and took part in a regular exercise program lost just as much fat as those who ate 1,200 calories and didn't exercise, according to *Food and Nutrition Research News Briefs.* Extra weight loss in the lower calorie group came from fluid and muscle tissue.(7)

Another study of women on a controlled low-calorie diet showed that their bodies used the calories more efficiently to provide energy, which made them lose weight more slowly, during the first five weeks. However, between five and fourteen weeks, those who exercised used up more calories to produce the same amount of energy and lost more fat.(7)

REFERENCES

1. Bonnie S. Worthington-Roberts, "The Fat Soluble Vitamins A and D," *Contemporary Developments in Nutrition* (St. Louis, MO: C. R. Mosby Company, 1981), 161, 166, 171–173, 188.

2. Diane Hubbard Burns, "After Dieting, You Should Watch Scales." Information from Dr. Wayne Callaway was reported by Diane Hubbard Burns in the *Orlando Sentinel* and the *Fort Worth Star Telegram,* January 6, 1988, Section 4, page 1.

3. William Bennett, M.D., and Joel Gurin, *The Dieter's Dilemma* (New York: Basic Books, Inc., 1982), 8, 11–16, 84, 87, 239, 259–261.

4. *Food, The Yearbook of Agriculture* (Washington, D.C.: United States Government Printing Office, 1959), 103.

5. Kelly Brownell, Ph.D., "The Effects of Repeated Cycles of Weight Loss and Regain in Rats," *Physiol. Behavior* 38 (1986): 459–464.

6. Diane L. Elliot, Linn Goldberg, Kerry S. Kuehl, and William M. Bennett, "Sustained Depression of the Resting Metabolic Rate after Massive Weight Loss," *American Journal of Clinical Nutrition* 49, no. 1 (January 1989): 93–96.

7. Jo Ann Vachule, "Short Orders: Diet Needs Exercise," *Fort Worth Star Telegram,* February 18, 1987, 2BB (information from *Food and Nutrition Research News Briefs*).

8. Djoeke Van Dale and Wim H. M. Saris, "Repetitive Weight Loss and Weight Regain Effects on Weight Reduction, Resting Metabolic Rate, and Lipolytic Activity Before and After Exercise and/or Treatment," *American Journal of Clinical Nutrition* 49, no. 3 (March 1989): 409–416.

6.

Menu Magic: Two Weeks of Menus with Alternatives

Use the following menus designed with approximately 1,200 calories, 4 bread exchanges, 3 fruit exchanges, 2 milk exchanges, 2–3 vegetable exchanges, and 6 oz. meat, fish, cheese or eggs, or look below for guidelines to make your own choices. Follow amounts allowed for the food plan you choose and be sure to use foods from each group which are good sources of the basic nutrients. Foods high in vitamin A or C are marked for each food group in the list of recommended serving amounts in Appendix B.

Alternate menus are listed across from each day's menu. If the foods you replace are good sources of Vitamin A, Vitamin C, or calcium, the alternative should be high in the same nutrients. Eggs and red meat should be limited to 3–4 servings per week. You can trade one day's menu for another in the same week. (Recipes for many of the dishes are in Chapter 1.)

Guidelines for Good Nutrition

Bread and cereals, starchy vegetables — 4–6 servings daily. (Diabetics should avoid more than 2 per meal.)

Fruits and vegetables — 5–6 servings daily (at least 1 citrus fruit or tomato and at least 1 dark green or yellow vegetable).

Milk — 2–4 servings daily, women need 3–4 to avoid osteoporosis.
Meat, eggs, fish — 6 oz. daily (2 sm. servings or a 4 oz. and a 2 oz.)

WEEK ONE

SUNDAY

(calories listed beside items)

Menus	***Alternative Menus***
Breakfast	
1/2 grapefruit 40	1/2 c. orange or grapefruit juice (unsweetened) 48–55
Oatmeal (no sugar added) 75	3/4 c. cold cereal (no sugar) 100 or 3/4 cup cream of wheat 105
1/2 c. skim milk (for cereal) 43	1/2 c. skim milk 43
Coffee, tea (no sugar or cream added)	
Above beverages allowed with any meal	
Dinner	
Marinated shishkabobs 390	One-dish Supper (beef, macaroni) 270
1/3 c. rice 74	1/2 c. cut green beans 18
1/2 c. cooked spinach 28	1 carrot cut in sticks 42
1 small tomato, sliced 26	1 c. skim milk 85
1 small apple 80	1 banana 105
Coffee, tea (no sugar or cream added)	
Supper	
Potato Soup (use our recipe or make canned with skim milk) 225	Canned bean soup 170
6 Saltine type crackers 75	Buttered toast 115
1/2 c. skim milk 43	3/4 c. lowfat cottage cheese 150
1/4 c. tuna (water-packed) 135	
1/3 c. pineapple, canned in juice 50	
Day's Total 1,284	Day's Total 1,251–1,258

MONDAY

Menus	***Alternative Menus***
Breakfast	
1 egg, cooked without fat 80	1/2 c. hot or 3/4 c. cold cereal (no sugar) 75–120
1 piece buttered toast 115	1/2 c. skim milk 43
Simply Fruit jam 16	1/2 banana 53
3/4 c. tomato juice 30	1/2 c. orange juice 55

Lunch

Sandwich (1 oz. turkey, lettuce, tomato, light mayo.) 258
1 c. skim milk 85
Ambrosia 107

Dinner

Chicken 'N Spice 217
1/2 c. cooked cauliflower 15
1/2 c. cooked broccoli 25
Two-way Bread Pudding 145-150
1 c. skim milk 85

Day's Total 1,178–1,183

Sandwich (1 oz. chicken, tomato, lettuce, light mayo.) 275
1/2 c. cottage cheese 63
2 peach halves 80

Chicken 'N Peppers 208
1/2 c. cooked cabbage 15
1/2 c. cooked green beans 23
1 c. skim milk 85
Carrot Cake (our recipe) 176

Day's Total 1,149–1,196

TUESDAY

Menus

Breakfast

3/4 c. cream of wheat 105
1 c. skim milk 85
1/2 banana 53
3/4 c. tomato juice 30

Lunch

Sandwich (1 oz. chicken, light mayo., lettuce, tomato) 275
1 c. skim milk 85
1 carrot, cut into sticks 42
Ambrosia 107

Dinner

Quick Herbed Chicken 233
1/2 c. cooked spinach 28
1/2 c. cooked beets 28
Black Forest Parfait 116

Day's Total 1,187

Alternative Menus

Poached egg, buttered toast 200
Diet jelly 16
1/2 grapefruit 40
1 c. skim milk 85

Sandwich (1 oz. turkey, tomato, lettuce, light mayo.) 245
Lowfat yogurt (8 oz.) 90
1 tomato, sliced 25
1 banana 105

Chicken with Wild Rice 232
1/2 c. cooked summer squash 18
Green beans and mushrooms 68

Day's Total 1,124

WEDNESDAY

Menus

Breakfast

3/4 c. cold cereal, 90–110
1/2 banana 53
1/2 c. skim milk 43
1/2 c. grapefruit juice 48

Alternative Menus

1/2 c. oatmeal (no sugar) 75
1/2 c. skim milk 43
1/2 c. orange juice 55

Lunch

Sandwich (1 oz. turkey, light mayo., lettuce, tomato) 245
1 small apple 80
1 c. skim milk 85

Sandwich (veal loaf lunchmeat, light mayo., lettuce, tomato) 275
1/2 banana 53
1 Spiced Tea Cake 61
3/4 c. lowfat cottage cheese 105

Dinner

Chicken Italian 271
1/2 c. cooked carrots 35
Key Lime Pudding 183

Day's Total 1,133–1,153

Lamb Burritos 303
1/2 c. cooked spinach 28
Peach Tapioca 174
1 c. skim milk 85

Day's Total 1,257

THURSDAY

Menus

Breakfast

3/4 c. cream of wheat 105
2 Tbs. raisins 54
1/2 c. grapefruit juice 48
1/2 c. skim milk for cereal 43

Lunch

Garden Chicken Salad 215
6 Saltine squares 75
1 carrot, cut in sticks 42 (the alternate is cantaloupe)
Vicki's Pineapple Frosty 93
1 c. skim milk 85

Dinner

One-dish supper (beef, macaroni) 270
1/2 c. cooked broccoli 25
Carolyn's Light Cheesecake 166

Day's Totals 1,221

Alternative Menus

1/2 c. oatmeal (no sugar) 75
1 c. skim milk 85
1/2 c. orange juice 55
1/3 cantaloupe 63

Sandwich (1 oz. chicken, light mayo., lettuce, tomato) 275 (use only 1 piece bread if you want cheesecake at supper)
1 c. skim milk 85
1/2 c. coleslaw 50

Maxi Dish — Beef, Rice, Beans 323
Mushroom Florentina 63
1 small apple 80

Day's Totals 1,154

FRIDAY

Menus	*Alternative Menus*
Breakfast	
1 egg (cooked without fat) 80	1/2 c. cooked oatmeal 72
1 piece bacon (crisp) 37	1/2 c. skim milk 43
1 piece dry toast, diet jelly 81	1/2 grapefruit 40
1/2 c. skim milk 43	
3/4 c. tomato juice 30	
Lunch	
1 c. Vegetable Beef Soup 80	New England Clam Chowder (made with skim milk) 172
6 Saltine squares 75	1 piece dry toast, diet jelly 81
1 c. skim milk 85	1 small apple 80
1 medium orange 60	
Dinner	
Fish Florentine 136	Scalloped Tuna 165
Mugwumps 132	1/2 c. cooked spinach 28
1/2 c. Swiss Green Beans 117	Asparagus Casserole 308
Lite Perfection Salad (#2) 30	Key Lime Pie 278
Applesauce Delight 157	
Day's Totals 1,143	**Day's Totals 1,267**

SATURDAY

Menus	*Alternative Menus*
Breakfast	
3/4 c. tomato juice 30	1/2 grapefruit 40
2 Apple Cranberry Muffins 304	2 Oat Bran Muffins 222
	1 c. skim milk 85
Lunch	
Nine Bean Soup 128	Canned bean with bacon soup 170
1 piece buttered toast 115	3 Saltine squares 38
1 carrot cut in sticks 42	1/2 c. lowfat cottage cheese 103
1 c. skim milk 85	15 small grapes 53
1 small apple 80	
Dinner	
Crispy Baked Chicken 235	Chicken 'N Spice 217
Pizza Plant (eggplant casserole) 140	1/2 c. cooked green beans 23
1/2 c. cooked spinach 28	1 carrot cut in sticks 42
Vicki's Pineapple Frosty 93	1 Orange Cranberry Nut Bar 211
Day's Totals 1,280	**Day's Totals 1,204**

WEEK TWO

SUNDAY

Menus	***Alternative Menus***
Breakfast	
3/4 c. cold cereal 90–110 1 c. skim milk 85 1/2 banana 53 3/4 c. tomato juice 30	3/4 c. cream of wheat 105 1 c. skim milk 85 1/2 c. strawberries 23 1/2 c. pineapple grapefruit juice 59
Dinner	
Chicken with Lemon Gravy 187 1/2 c. cooked carrots 23 1/2 c. Peas and Asparagus Casserole 112 Peach Tapioca 174	Fish Florentine 136 1/2 c. cooked broccoli 25 Oriental Green Beans 146 Key Lime Pudding 183
Supper	
1 c. Nine Bean Soup 128 Buttered toast 115 Black Forest Parfait 116 1 c. skim milk 85	1 c. Steak Soup 213 Oat Bran Muffin 111 Delightfully Tropical 31 1 c. skim milk 85
Day's Totals 1,198–1,218	Day's totals 1,202

MONDAY

Menus	***Alternative Menus***
Breakfast	
1 egg (cooked without fat) 85 1 piece bacon (crisp) 37 1 piece toast (diet jelly) 81 1/2 c. orange juice 55 1 c. skim milk 85	1/2 grapefruit 40 1/2 c. oatmeal 75 1 c. skim milk 85
Lunch	
Sandwich (1 oz. chicken, light mayo., lettuce, tomato) 275 1 c. skim milk 85 1 small apple 80	Sandwich (veal loaf lunchmeat, light mayo., lettuce, tomato) 275 1 slice process lite cheese 90 1 small pear 85

Dinner

Chicken With Wild Rice 157	Chicken Spaghetti 262
1 c. cooked spinach 55	Broccoli Casserole 161
Light Perfection Salad (#2) 30	Cucumber Gazpacho 108
Banana Pudding 136	Strawberries Romanoff 57
Day's Totals 1,161	**Day's totals 1,238**

TUESDAY

Menus	***Alternative Menus***
Breakfast	
1/2 c. oatmeal 73	1/2 c. cream of wheat 70
1/2 c. skim milk 43	1 c. skim milk 85
1/2 banana 53	2 Tbs. raisins 54
Lunch	
Sandwich (1 oz. turkey, lettuce, tomato, light mayo.) 245	Sandwich (1 oz. chicken, lettuce, tomato, light mayo.) 275
1 c. skim milk 85	1/2 c. lowfat cottage cheese 103
1 medium orange 60	1/2 grapefruit 40
Self-dressed Salad 47	Spinach Salad (tomato, dressing) 30
Dinner	
Spinach Lasagna 407	Chicken 'N Spice 217
Broccoli Cauliflower Dish 45	Pizza Plant 140
1/2 c. cooked carrots 23	Cheese Potatoes 176
Lime Parfait 87	Delightfully Tropical 31
Day's Totals 1,168	**Day's Totals 1,221**

WEDNESDAY

Menus	***Alternative Menus***
Breakfast	
Cold cereal (no sugar) 110	1/2 c. oatmeal 73
1/2 banana 53	1 Tbs. raisins 30
1 c. skim milk 85	1 c. skim milk 85
3/4 c. tomato juice 30	1/2 c. grapefruit juice 48
Lunch	
1 c. Vegetable Beef Soup 80	1 c. Bean With Bacon Soup 170
Dry toast 65	3 Saltine crackers 38
1 c. skim milk 85	1/2 c. lowfat cottage cheese 103
1/2 c. peaches (juice pack) 55	1 small apple 80

Dinner

Piquant Baked Chicken 183
Swissed Green Beans 117
Marinated Eggplant Salad 134
Apricot Custard Pie 247

Day's Totals 1,244

Lasagna 397
Light Perfection Salad 56
1/2 c. cooked zucchini 18
Frozen Fruit Fun Dessert 47

Day's Totals 1,145

THURSDAY

Menus

Breakfast

1 egg scrambled without fat 80
Buttered toast with diet jelly 131
1 piece crisp bacon 38
1 c. skim milk 85

Lunch

Garden Chicken Salad 144
1 carrot cut in sticks 42
Ambrosia 66
1 c. skim milk 85

Dinner

Nine Bean Soup 128
6 Saltine squares 75
Summer Salad 56
Carrot Cake 176

Day's Totals 1,106

Alternative Menus

1 poached egg on dry toast 145
1/2 c. grapefruit juice 48
2 c. lite hot chocolate made with 1 c. skim milk 104

Tuna Salad 131 (sub. tuna for chicken)
Cucumber Gazpacho 108
1 Light Coconut Bar 90
1 c. skim milk 85
1/3 cantaloupe 64

Steak Soup 213
1 piece dry toast 65
Self-dressed Salad 47
2 Banana Oatmeal Cookies 91

Day's Totals 1,191

FRIDAY

Menus

Breakfast

1/2 c. cream of wheat 70
2 Tbs. raisins 54
1 c. skim milk 85
1/2 c. orange juice 55

Lunch

Salmon Treat Salad 125
3 Saltine squares 38
1 c. skim milk 85
Diet gelatin with 1/2 banana 60

Alternative Menus

1 c. cold cereal (no sugar) 110 with 1 Tbs. raisins 27
1 c. skim milk 85
1/2 grapefruit 40

Tomato Half Stuffed With Garden Chicken Salad 228
1/2 c. lowfat cottage cheese 103
Cola Fruit Salad 50
1 piece buttered toast 115

Dinner

Fish with Wild Rice 430
1/2 c. green beans 23
1 carrot cut in sticks 42
Two-Way Bread Pudding 144

Day's Totals 1,211

Scalloped Tuna 165
1/2 c. cooked broccoli 25
Spinach 28
Carrot Cake (our recipe) 174
1 c. skim milk 85

Day's Totals 1,235

SATURDAY

Menus

Breakfast

Banana Classic Coffee Cake 291
1 c. skim milk 85
3/4 c. tomato juice 30

Lunch

Spiral Veggie Casserole 166
3 Saltine squares 38
1/2 grapefruit 40
1/2 c. skim milk 43

Dinner

Chicken 'N Peppers 208
Swissed Green Beans 117
1/2 c. cooked spinach 28
Lime Parfait 84

Day's Totals 1,130

Alternative Menus

2 Microwave Applesauce Muffins 236
1 c. nonfat yogurt (Dannon) 110
1/2 c. orange juice 55

1 c. cream of mushroom soup (make with skim milk) 130
1 piece buttered toast 115
Chocolate Roll 103

Crispy Baked Chicken 235
1/2 c. cooked carrots 35
8 boiled whole okra 25
Our Lemon Pie 144

Day's Totals 1,188

7.

Tips to Make Healthy Eating Easier

TIPS FOR EATING OUT

1. **The salad bar is a good choice, but beware!** Avoid creamy dressings, cheese, deviled eggs, bacon, ham, and gelatin salads with whipped cream. Use vinaigrette or oil and vinegar dressing in a side dish. Don't pour dressing on salad. Dip your fork in it before you take a bite of salad.

2. **Baked potatoes have only 100–150 calories, but** — watch out for all that butter at 100 calories per tablespoon. Sour cream, cheese, and bacon bits are almost as bad.

3. **Chicken is good for you unless it's fried or you eat the skin.** Next time you prepare chicken, pull the skin off and look at all that fat sticking to the underside of it.

4. **Ask how many ounces are in the steak.** A 7-oz. steak is slightly more than your daily requirement for meat. Even with visible fat trimmed off, a good steak has tiny streaks of fat marbled through it. Some doctors advise against red meat for this reason.

5. **Look for low-calorie items.** Ask for substitutions for French fries and high-calorie items. Most restaurants have sliced tomatoes and cottage cheese available. If not, ask for a serving of vegetable.

6. **Drink lots of water with your meal to help fill you up.**

7. **Avoid cream soups.** Many are made with lots of cream and butter. Choose soup made with clear broth instead.

8. **Don't order something fattening and say you will eat only part of it — you are only kidding yourself.**

9. **Do not order dessert.** Made with real butter and whipped cream, they are designed to be appealing, not low-calorie. Let someone else order one and give you just a bite. Sometimes one bite helps satisfy the craving. If you can't resist dessert, split it with someone. Eating half the calories is better than eating them all.

10. **Choose the lowest calorie items at fast food places.**

Arby's: pick Roast Beef — 350 cal., 15 g. fat instead of Super Roast Beef — 620 cal., 28 g. fat

Dairy Queen: pick Fish Sandwich — 400 cal., 17 g. fat instead of Super Hot Dog & Chili — 570 cal., 27 g. fat

Long John Silver's: pick 2 pieces Fish with Batter — 366 Cal., 22 g. fat instead of Breaded Clams — 617 cal., 34 g. fat

McDonald's: pick Chicken McNuggets — 332 cal., 19 g. fat instead of Cheese Quarter Pounder — 524 cal., 31 g. fat

Pizza Hut: pick Standard Pepperoni pizza — 430 cal., 19 g. fat instead of Super Supreme Pizza — 520 cal., 26 g. fat (1)

Wendy's: pick Chili — 260 cal, 8 g. fat instead of Double Burger with Cheese — 560 cal., 40 g. fat (2)

11. **If you overeat — resolve not to do it again!** Then exercise for half an hour (heart patients, consult doctor first) and cut down on calories for the rest of the day and the next.

Some folks are allergic to ice cream; it makes their hips swell!

WAYS TO CUT CALORIES YOU WON'T EVEN MISS

12. **For coffee and tea** — Use saccharin and milk instead of cream in coffee. (Some powdered cream substitutes with less calories taste good, but many have corn syrup solids not recommended for diabetics or are made with coconut oil, considered by some as harmful as beef fat.) Learn to drink it black.

13. **Use diet margarine with half the calories of regular margarine.** Even if you use a little more, you save calories.

14. **Slice banana on cereal and skip the sugar.** You need fruit and banana supplies needed potassium.

15. **Use NutraSweet on dry cereal or cooked cereal.**

16. **Drink diet colas.** Twelve ounces of Pepsi has ten teaspoons sugar (160 calories) and Coke has 9.8.

17. **Refrigerate soups and stews to congeal fat.** It collects on top and hardens so you can easily lift it off and reheat food.

18. **In recipes calling for two whole eggs, use 2 egg whites instead of the second whole egg.** If you feel that's wasteful, give egg yolks to the dog or throw it out — it's better for it to go to *waste* than to *waist.*

19. **Cook with skim milk and nonfat powdered milk instead of whole.** When a recipe calls for 1 cup milk, use 1/3 cup powdered milk and 1 cup cold water. Add skim milk to pudding mixes, cake mixes, or soup instead of whole milk. (Skim milk has 86 calories per cup; whole milk has 166.)

20. **Eat ice milk instead of ice cream for one-third less calories.**

21. **Use a butter flavor such as Molly McButter or Adams Imitation Butter Flavoring instead of butter.** Good with instant mashed potatoes. Check label; avoid those heavy in sodium. Use sparingly. Some have strong flavors.

22. **Use tomato, lemon, or even pickle juice (not from sweet ones) instead of salad dressing.** Try fat-free diet dressings.

23. **Thicken sauces with cornstarch instead of flour.** Cornstarch is easier to mix with cold liquid. One tablespoon of cornstarch will make a sauce as thick as 2 tablespoons of flour, using only half the calories.

24. **Use cocoa instead of squares of chocolate and skip the 1/2 tsp. of fat recommended in substitution.** Use less chocolate or cocoa than the recipe calls for; the dish will taste sweeter and you can cut down on sugar.

25. **Don't put butter or margarine on vegetables before serving.** Family members can add some if desired.

26. **Use Equal or SugarTwin to sweeten something that won't be cooked.** Some sweeteners break down when heated a long time.

27. **Use thin diet bread or freeze a regular piece to make it easier to cut a slice in two layers for a sandwich.**

28. **Chew sugar-free gum instead of eating a snack.**

29. **Use lowfat yogurt instead of sour cream on baked potatoes.** Substitute lowfat yogurt for half of mayonnaise in salad dressing.

30. **Substitute lowfat yogurt for sour cream in dip recipes.**

31. **Serve a low-calorie dip with raw vegetables when entertaining.** Fill up on that before tasting anything fattening. When entertaining, make only enough for one meal. Give leftover dessert to guests to take home.

32. **Drain browned hamburger in a colander or on paper towel.**

33. **Bake appetizer meatballs on broiler pan so grease will drip off while they cook.**

34. **Make your own sherbet.** Prepare diet Jell-o (add saccharin with the hot water if it isn't sweet enough) and freeze. When it's solid, put it in blender or beat with a mixer.

35. **Keep only things that have to be cooked.** It will seem like too much trouble to get something ready to eat when it's not mealtime.

36. **Season popcorn with Weight Watcher's Butter-flavored Vegetable Spray** and sprinkle on No Salt instead of using butter and salt for about 100 calories per cup.

37. **Add a little skim milk to regular milk,** and keep increasing the amount you add until you get used to drinking plain skim milk. That will cut your milk calories in half.

38. **If you are tempted to eat something else after your meal, eat fruit** — and wait twenty minutes. According to Judith Wurtman, Ph.D., when someone eats carbohydrates (starchy or sweet food), it takes 20 minutes to digest. Then the brain makes serotonin, which makes you feel good.

39. **Use plain graham crackers or saltines.** The extra good crackers often have a lot of fat and calories.

APPENDIX A

YOU CAN'T KNOW THE PLAYERS WITHOUT A SCORECARD: The Lowdown on All Those Complicated-sounding Names for Fat

It is almost impossible to avoid eating some fat. Your body uses a small amount to promote growth, keep warm, and make cell walls and hormones. The rest is stored in fat cells to protect against starvation. This is the last energy resource your body uses, which is why it takes so long to get rid of bulges. When you exercise vigorously, that uses up your stored carbohydrates so that energy must come from fat cells.

Doctors say too much fat increases the risk of heart attacks. Then they talk about saturated fat, unsaturated fat, monounsaturated fat, serum cholesterol, triglycerides, low density lipoproteins (LDL), and high-density lipoproteins (HDL) until you don't know what to believe. Look below to see those terms unmasked.

Adipose Tissue: Fat cells; mini-warehouses to hide fat-stuff you're not using — just in case you might need it someday if threatened with starvation. When you exercise vigorously, your body uses up stored glycogen (a form of starch made in the liver from carbohydrates you eat). Then your body draws on the fat cells for energy.(1) Scientists believe that the number of fat cells developed by adulthood stays the same, and that fat cells swell to accumulate more fat and shrink when they release it for energy.

Atherosclerosis: Hardening of the arteries — when fat particles plaster themselves to the inside of your blood vessels. Your heart must work harder, and you might have a heart attack.

Cholesterol: A villain dressed in creamy white. Remember when you were a teenager and got whiteheads? Those are made of cholesterol. That nasty stuff sticks to the inside of your blood vessel walls. It traps metallic and other substances from your blood to make a briar patch, which your blood has to try to get through somehow. Deep in your body a secret laboratory manufactures cholesterol naturally, but you want to avoid adding to it by eating foods high in cholesterol. See SERUM CHOLESTEROL.

Fat: A high-calorie substance, found in solid or liquid form or hidden in other foods. Often cast as a villain causing obesity and heart attacks, some fat is necessary for good health. Fatty compounds are important for cell membrane development. Fat keeps you warm, carries vitamins A, D, and K, and helps make hormones for growth, sexual maturity, pregnancy, and lactation.(1) Fat provides flavor, makes foods more tender, and helps you feel satisfied after eating because it takes longer to digest.

Young women on diets severely low in fat may have irregular menstrual periods and experience difficulty in becoming pregnant.

Heredity: The hand that's dealt you at birth — who said life was fair? Some people's fat cells can't absorb as many LDLs (See Low-density Lipoproteins and High-density Lipoproteins), which allows too many of those "banty roosters" to circulate in the blood. The ratio of HDL to LDL, the amount of triglycerides and total cholesterol in the blood should all be checked by a doctor to judge your risk of heart attack.

HDLs or High-density Lipoproteins: Elephant-size molecules of protein with fat attached. If you have enough HDL "elephants" compared to the number of LDL "banty roosters" (low-density lipoproteins), the "elephants" will act as cops to avoid traffic jams in your blood stream and protect you from heart attacks.(2)

Several theories exist to explain the relationship between the "elephants" and the "banty roosters." One maintains that the "elephant" HDLs block absorption of the "banty rooster" LDLs by the cell walls of the arteries. Another theory is that the "elephant" molecules herd the free "banty roosters" back to the fat cells. It's possible that a crowd of "elephant" molecules in the serum cholesterol means that there aren't as many loose LDL "banty roosters" brave enough to run around causing trouble.

Lipid: Another name for fat.

Lipoproteins: In order to dissolve in the blood, a fat hooks up with a protein like a Siamese twin and the result is called a lipoprotein.

Low-density Lipoprotein: Often called LDLs, these are the "banty rooster" molecules of fat and protein that fat cells use to make cell membranes and store for extra energy. "Banty rooster" molecules running loose can hide in your artery walls to cause trouble later.

Monounsaturated Fats: Oils like a little boy with all of his pockets filled but one (he is saving that for a snake). Olive oil is a monounsaturated fat. These fats get rid of many of the "banty rooster" LDLs like polyunsaturated fats do, but they don't scare away the good "elephant" HDLs.

Partially Hyrdrogenated Fats: See polyunsaturated fats below. Partially hydrogenated fats are naturally unsaturated fats that have had some of the pockets filled with hydrogen, which makes them more like saturated fats. Some peanut butters are made this way.

Polyunsaturated Fats: These fats are like a little boy with lots of empty pockets that can be filled with more hydrogen. Unsaturated fats are liquid at room temperature and usually come from plants.

Saturated Fats: These fats are like a little boy with his pockets stuffed, in this case with all the hydrogen that they can hold. Saturated fats are solid at room temperature and found mostly in animal foods such as eggs, butter, and meat. However, some plant foods are highly saturated. For example: palm oil and coconut oil. Your body can easily convert these to cholesterol and triglycerides in the body,(2) so avoid these bad actors.

Serum Cholesterol: Dissolved cholesterol floating around loose in your bloodstream. Generally, a rating under 200 means you're in good shape, but your weight, blood pressure, triglycerides, and HDL to LDL ratio should all be checked by a doctor to be sure.

Triglycerides: Free-floating, undigested fat looking for a place to cause trouble in blood or cells.

Unsaturated Fats: Fats with empty pockets that can hold more hydrogen. Most unsaturated fats are liquid at room temperature and are usually found in plant foods. However, some plant foods such as palm oil, coconut oil, cocoa butter, and chocolate are highly saturated. Most of the fats you eat should be unsaturated.

Even unsaturated fat should be eaten sparingly! According to Richard Phillips of the *Chicago Tribune,* as quoted in the *Dallas Morning News* on October 18, 1987, too much polyunsaturated fat tends to cause narrowing of the arteries, blood clots, and possibly cancer of the breast, urinary tract, and prostate.

Very Low-density Lipoproteins: The Cornish hens of cholesterol; so little they escape easily and hide in your blood vessels to cause trouble later.

REFERENCES

1. Bonnie S. Worthington-Roberts, "Diet and Athletic Performance," "Questions Related to Dietary Fats," and "The Fat Soluble Vitamins A and D," *Contemporary Developments in Nutrition* (St. Louis, MO: C. V. Mosby Company, 1981), 77, 84–89, 161, 166.

2. Kenneth Cooper, M.D., M.P.H, *Controlling Cholesterol* (New York: Bantam Books, 1988), 22–34, 77–80.

APPENDIX B

DIABETIC FOOD EXCHANGES

Eat the recommended number of servings from the six food groups. Each group contains foods with similar amounts of protein, carbohydrates, fats and calories. The groups are A. Milk and Cheese, B. Meat, Eggs and Fish, C. Breads, D. Fruits, E. Vegetables, and F. Fats.

Check the following lists of foods allowed to find out how much a serving is. Weigh or measure the first few times until you can judge the correct amount by looking. A list of Free Foods you can eat anytime follows the food groups lists.

Nutritious menus are provided in Chapter 6. Or you can choose your own foods by following the guidelines for good nutrition in this section. When you eat less calories, it is very important to eat foods with enough protein, vitamins and minerals. Be sure to choose enough milk, a vitamin A rich vegetable or fruit (marked with an "A"), a vitamin C rich food (marked with a "C"), and some food rich in fiber (marked with an "f") each day.

SERVING SIZES AND FOODS IN THE SIX FOOD GROUPS

A. Milk group: Eat 2–4 exchanges daily.

Milk provides protein to keep your body in good repair and calcium to keep bones and teeth sturdy. Choose skim milk or milk with 1/2% milk fat. Whole milk has too much cholesterol and fat. While cheese also provides protein and calcium, it is in the meat group because it is higher in fat and calories.

Calcium loss from bones begins at 25. Women who skimp on milk risk osteroporosis (brittle bones) in later years. (Skim milk with 86 calories and no fat per glass has the same amount of calcium as regular milk at 166 calories with 3.5–4% fat.)

Thin women who smoke, don't exercise, haven't eaten enough calcium-rich foods and don't take estrogen supplements, if needed, are likely to get osteoporosis. A four-year study done by Dr. Kewis Kuller of 174 healthy women past menopause indicates taking calcium and exercising after fifty doesn't help as much as getting adequate calcium all your life.

MILK GROUP SERVING SIZES

Milk Group — Each Serving Listed Provides 1 Milk Serving

1 cup skim milk, 1/2% buttermilk, 1%, 2% milk, or whole milk
1/2 cup evaporated milk
1/3 cup dry nonfat powdered milk
8 oz. lowfat or regular yogurt
(One milk group serving has approx. 12 g. carbohydrate, 8 g. protein, 0 to 8 g. fat, and 86 to 166 calories.)

B. Meat, fish, eggs, and cheese group: Eat at least 5 or more meat group serving units daily.

1 oz. of meat = 1 meat exchange (average 3 oz. serving = 3 serving units). One meat group unit has 7 g. protein, 3–8 g. fat, and 55–100 calories.

Eat less red meat! Everyone interested in living longer — and who isn't? — should eat foods with animal fats in small amounts and less often. Three to four ounces of meat is enough for one meal. Six ounces of meat a day combined with a balanced diet provides plenty of protein. Choose mostly chicken without skin, turkey, and fish.

MEAT GROUP SERVING UNITS
(Each amount listed provides 1 meat unit.)

Beef: ground beef, roasts, steaks, corned beef	1 oz.
Pork: ham, Canadian bacon, pork chops, roast	1 oz.
Veal: chops, roasts	1 oz.
Poultry: chicken, turkey, Cornish hen (without skin)	1 oz.
Fish: fish	1 oz.
crab, lobster, scallops, clams, shrimp	2 oz.
oysters	6 medium
tuna (canned in water)	1/4 cup
Wild game: venison, rabbit, squirrel, pheasant, duck, goose (without skin)	1 oz.
Eat these high fat meats 3 or fewer times per week:	
Luncheon meat: bologna, salami, pimento loaf	1 oz.
Sausage: Polish, Italian, knockwurst, bratwurst	1 oz.
Hot dog: turkey or chicken (ten per pound)	1 hot dog
beef or pork hot dogs (add 1 fat exchange)	1 hot dog
Bacon: (listed in the fats group)	
Eggs	1

One egg with 213 mg. of cholesterol takes up almost all the recommended daily limit of 300 mg. cholesterol for normal persons, so limit whole eggs to 3–4 per week.

Cheese: Good cheeses are lowfat cottage cheese, ricotta cheese made with skim milk, mozzarella cheese and pot cheese. Read labels. Compare Kraft's low-calorie process cheese with 4 g. of fat per 1 oz. serving to Borden's light cheese with 2 g. of fat per oz.

cottage cheese	1/4 cup
grated parmesan	2 Tbs.
diet cheese (50–80 calories per oz.)	1 oz.
skim or part skim cheeses:	
ricotta	1/4 cup
mozzarella	1 oz.
hard cheeses (eat only 3 or less times/week) (American, Swiss, Monterey, cheddar)	1 oz.

C. Breads: Eat at least 3–4 servings daily.

This includes bread, rice, potatoes, noodles, beans, etc. For low-calorie diets, choose breads and cereals enriched with iron, niacin, thiamin, and riboflavin. Diabetics should watch the number and size of bread servings carefully, and those on low-calorie diets should limit themselves to four–five servings daily. The following foods equal one bread unit in the amounts shown. An "f" next to the item means it is high in fiber. Each unit from the bread group gives you approximately 3 g. of protein, 15 g. of carbohydrate, a trace of fat, and 80 calories.

BREAD GROUP SERVING SIZES

(Each amount listed is one bread serving.)

Cereals

Bran cereals, (f) concentrated (Bran Buds, All Bran)	1/3 cup
Bran cereals, (f) flakes	1/2 cup
Cooked cereals (oatmeal, cream of wheat)	1/2 cup
Cornmeal, dry	2½ Tbs.
Most unsweetened dry cereals	3/4 cup
Pasta, cooked (spaghetti, egg noodles, macaroni etc.)	1/2 cup
Rice (white or brown, cooked)	1/3 cup
Shredded wheat	1/2 cup
Wheat germ (f)	3 Tbs.

Dried beans, peas, lentils

Beans, black-eyed peas, split peas, kidney beans, navy beans, white beans, lentils (cooked) (all f)	1/3 cup
Baked beans (f)	1/4 cup

Carbohydrates as a source of protein. Complete proteins (meat, eggs, fish, milk, cheese) have all eight essential amino acids. If you eat foods rich in the eight essential amino acids, your body can make the other twelve amino acids you need to build muscles and repair tissues. A serving of beans or grains only has some of the necessary eight amino acids and needs to be supplemented with a food that supplies the rest, such as a complete protein or a complementary food. The following combinations provide complete protein when served in one meal:

1. beans, peas, or lentils and a kind of grain (wheat, rice)
2. beans, peas, or lentils and nuts or seeds (sunflower seeds, etc.)

Starchy Vegetables

Corn (f)	1/2 cup
Corn on the cob, 6 inches long (f)	1 ear
Lima beans (f)	1/2 cup
Peas, green (canned or frozen) (A, f)	1/2 cup
Potato, baked or boiled	1 small
Potato, mashed	1/2 cup
Squash, winter (A) (acorn, butternut)	3/4 cup
Yams, (A) (sweet potato)	1/3 cup

Bread

Bagel	1/2 (1 oz.)
Breadsticks, crisp (4 x 1/2")	2 (2/3 oz.)
Croutons, lowfat	1 cup
English muffin	1/2
Hamburger or hot dog bun	1/2
Pita pocket bread (6" across)	1/2
Plain roll, small	1
Raisin bread without frosting	1 slice

Rye, (f) pumpernickel, white, whole wheat, French, Italian	1 slice
Tortilla (6" across)	1

Crackers, snacks

Graham crackers, plain	2 1/2" square
Matzos	3/4 oz.
Oyster crackers	24 crackers
Popcorn popped without fat	1 cup
Pretzels	3/4 oz.
Rye crisp, 2 x 3 1/2"	4
Saltine-type crackers	6
Whole wheat crackers	3

Starchy foods prepared with fat — count 1 bread and 1 fat

Biscuit, 2 1/2" across	1
Chow mein noodles	1/2 cup
Cornbread, 2" square	1 piece
French fries, 2"–3 1/2" long	10
Muffin, plain, small	1
Pancake, 4" across	1
Stuffing, bread	1/4 cup
Taco shell, 6" across	2
Waffle, 4 1/2" square	1
Whole wheat crackers with fat added (such as Triscuits)	5

Note: Croissants and Danish pastries are not included. A Dallas hotel pastry chef's instructions for making croissant dough were: weigh the yeast dough and add an equivalent weight of butter. No wonder they're so fattening!

D. Fruits and Vegetable Groups: Eat 4–6 servings daily.

Be sure to eat good sources of vitamin C and vitamin A daily. Vitamin C rich foods are citrus fruits (orange, grapefruits, lemons), tomatoes, cabbage, and strawberries. They are marked with a "C." Dark green, dark yellow, and orange vegetables marked with an "A" are good sources of vitamin A. Good examples are spinach and other greens, carrots, orange squash, broccoli, etc. Half of a cantaloupe has plenty vitamin A and only 25 calories.

FRUIT GROUP SERVING SIZES

Fruits, fresh, frozen, unsweetened canned (each amount = 1 fruit unit). Most servings are 1/2 cup of fruit or fruit juice or 1/4 cup dried fruit. Each fruit unit provides approximately 15 g. of carbohydrate and 60 calories.

Note: Fruits high in fiber are marked with an "f," fruits high in vitamin C are marked with a "C," and those high in vitamin A are marked with an "A."

Apple, raw, 2" across	1
Applesauce (unsweetened)	1/2 cup
Apricots, (A) medium, raw	4
canned	1/2 cup or 4 halves
Banana, 9" long	1/2 banana
Blackberries, (f) raw	3/4 cup

Blueberries, (f) raw	3/4 cup
Cantaloupe, 5″ across (A, C)	1/3 melon
cubes	1 cup
Cherries, (A) large, raw	12 cherries
Figs, raw, 2″ across	2 figs
Fruit cocktail (canned)	1/2 cup
Grapefruit, medium	1/2 grapefruit
Grapes, small	15 grapes
Honeydew melon, medium	1/8 melon
cubes	1 cup
Kiwi, large (C)	1 kiwi
Mandarin oranges (C)	3/4 cup
Nectarine, (A, f) 1½″ across	1 nectarine
Orange 2½″ inches across (C)	1 orange
Papaya (C)	1 cup
Peach, 2¾″ inches across	1 peach
Peaches, canned	1/2 cup or 2 halves
Pears	1/2 large or 1 small pear
canned	1/2 cup or 2 halves
Persimmon, medium	2 persimmons
Pineapple, raw	3/4 cup
canned	1/3 cup
Plum, (A) raw, 2″ across	2 plums
Pomegranate (f)	1/2 pomegranate
Raspberries, (C, f) raw	1 cup
Strawberries, (C, f) raw, whole	1¼ cups
Tangerine, (A, C) 2½ inches across	2 tangerines
Watermelon, (A, C) cubes	1¼ cups

Dried Fruit

Apples (f)	4 rings
Apricots (A, f)	7 halves
Dates	2½
Figs (f)	1½
Prunes (f)	3 medium
Raisins	2 Tbs.

Fruit Juice

Apple juice, cider	1/2 cup
Cranberry juice cocktail	1/3 cup
Grapefruit juice (C)	1/2 cup
Orange juice (C)	1/2 cup
Pineapple juice	1/2 cup
Prune juice	1/3 cup

E. Vegetables: Eat 2–4 servings daily.

Serving size for vegetables is 1/2 cup cooked vegetables, 1 cup raw vegetables, or 1/2 cup vegetable juice, such as tomato or V-8. Vegetables rich in vitamin A are marked with an "A." One serving from the vegetable group will provide approximately 5 g. of carbohydrate, 2 g. of protein, and 25 calories. Starchy vegetables are on the bread list, and low-carbohydrate vegetables are on the free foods list.

VEGETABLE SERVING SIZES

(1/2 cup of cooked vegetables or vegetable juice or 1 cup raw vegetable.)

Artichoke (1/2 medium)	Asparagus (A)
Beans, green, wax, Italian	Bean sprouts
Beets	Broccoli (A)
Brussels sprouts (A)	Cabbage (C)
Carrots (A)	Cauliflower (C)
Eggplant (A)	Greens, (A) collard (C), mustard, turnip, Swiss chard, kale (A, C)
Kohlrabi	Leeks
Mushrooms	Okra
Onions	Pea pods (snow peas)
Peppers, green	Rutabaga
Sauerkraut (A) (high in salt)	Spinach (A)
Summer squash	Tomato (A,C) (one large)
Tomato, V-8 juice (A, C) (high in salt)	Turnips
Water chestnuts	Zucchini

F. Fats: Limit to 1–9 servings daily, depending on food plan chosen. One serving of fat has approximately 5 g. fat and 45 calories.

Watch the Fat You Eat

Too much fat makes you unattractive and shortens your life!

Like most Americans, you probably get 40% of your calories from fat. Experts say you should cut down to 30% or even better, 10–15% (10% would mean cutting off all fat from meat before cooking, avoiding naturally fatty foods such as bacon, hot dogs, pork, some cheeses, fried foods, and eating only two pats of margarine a day).

Fat has 255 calories per ounce (9 calories/gram), protein and carbohydrates have only 113 calories per ounce (4 calories/gram).

While cutting down on total fat is important, it is even more important to choose carefully the kinds of fat you eat. Unsaturated fat (found mostly in plant foods and oils) is better for you than saturated fat (found in animal foods and fats that are solid at room temperature), which causes more cholesterol in your body. When cholesterol deposits build up on the walls of your arteries, that causes traffic jams in your bloodstreams, and can cause heart attacks, angina with its pain and shortness of breath, and *death at an early age.*(1)

For cooking, use the polyunsaturated fats, such as corn oil, safflower oil, sunflower oil and soybean oil, and monounsaturated fats such as olive oil and fish oil to help lower cholesterol in your blood. Peanut oil lowers cholesterol, but according to Robert Wissler, a University of Chicago pathologist, quoted in the *Dallas Morning News* on October 16, 1987, "There must be fifty papers in medical literature now that indicate peanut oil is unusually anthrogenic" (causes hardening of the arteries).(2)

For more about fat see page Appendix A.

Fat Servings

Each food listed counts as 1 fat.

Unsaturated Fats	
Avocado	1/8 of 1 medium
Margarine	1 tsp. (1 pat = 1½ tsp.)
Margarine, diet type	1 Tbs.
Mayonnaise	1 tsp.
Mayonnaise, reduced calorie	1 Tbs.
Nuts and seeds	
Almonds, dry roasted	6
Cashews, dry roasted	1 Tbs.
Pecans	2
Peanuts	20 small or 10 large
Walnuts	2
Other nuts	1 Tbs.
Seeds, pine nuts, sunflower seeds	1 Tbs.
Pumpkin seeds	2 tsp.
Oil, corn, cottonseed, safflower, soybean, sunflower, olive, peanut	1 tsp.
Salad dressing, mayonnaise type	2 tsp.
Salad dressing, mayonnaise type, reduced calorie	1 Tbs.
Salad dressing, all varieties	1 Tbs.
Salad dressing, reduced calorie	2 Tbs.
Saturated Fats (high in cholesterol, eat sparingly)	
Butter	1 tsp.
Bacon	1 slice
Coconut, shredded	2 Tbs.
Coffee creamer, liquid type	2 Tbs.
Coffee creamer, powder type	2 Tbs.
Cream, light	2 Tbs.
Cream, sour	2 Tbs.
Cream, heavy whipping	1 Tbs.
Cream cheese	1 Tbs.
Salt pork	1/4 oz.

Miscellaneous Exchanges

Exchanges for canned soups (made with milk or water)

Beef with veg., barley	1 cup	1/2 Bread, 1/2 Meat
Cream of chicken	1 cup	1/2 Bread, 1 Fat
Cream of mushroom	1 cup	1/2 Bread, 2 Fats
Cream of tomato	1 cup	1½ Bread
Chicken gumbo	1¼ cups	1/2 Bread
Chicken noodle, beef noodle	1 cup	1/2 Bread
Chicken with rice	1¼ cups	1/2 Bread, 1/2 Meat
Clam Chowder, milk style	1 cup	1 Milk, 1/2 Bread
French Onion Soup	1¼ cups	1 Bread
Green Pea	1 cup	1½ Bread, 1/2 Meat

Minestrone	$1^1/_4$ cups	1 Bread, 1/2 Meat
Split pea, ham, bacon	$1^1/_4$ cups	2 Bread, 1 Meat
Tomato	1 cup	1 Bread
Vegetable	1 cup	1 Bread
Vegetable beef	$1^1/_4$ cups	1/2 Bread, 1/2 Meat

Free Foods!

These foods have less than twenty calories per serving. If the serving size is shown, you can have it two or three times per day. You may eat all you want of the other foods.

Drinks:
Bouillon
Broth without fat
Carbonated drinks, sugar-free (3 per day)
Club soda
Cocoa powder, 1 Tbs., unsweetened
Coffee, tea
Kool-aid, sugar-free
Tonic water, sugar-free

Fruit:
Cranberries, 1/2 cup without sugar
Rhubarb, 1/2 cup without sugar

Salad greens:
Endive
Escarole
Lettuce
Romaine
Spinach

Vegetables (raw, 1 cup)

Cabbage
Chinese cabbage
Dill, sour pickles
Mushrooms
Zucchini
Celery
Cucumber
Green onion
Radishes

Sweets: (all sugar-free) hard candy, jam, jelly, gum, pancake syrup, gelatin

REFERENCES

1. Kenneth H. Cooper, M.D., M.P.H., *Controlling Cholesterol* (New York: Bantam Books, 1988), 18–21, 77, 80.

2. Richard Phillips, "Nothing But the Fats: Separating the Good From the Bad," *Dallas Morning News,* October 18, 1987.

3. American Diabetes Association, Inc., The American Dietetic Association, *Exchange Lists for Meal Planning,* American Diabetes Association, Inc., and the American Dietetic Association, 1986.

Index

About the Authors

Carolyn Williamson

Carolyn Williamson loves to create new recipes and to adapt rich dishes to tasty, more healthful ones.

Holding a master's degree in home economics, she has taught restaurant cooking, fancy cooking, home economics, and English in public schools and prisons, worked in hotels and restaurants, developed mincemeat formulas, and run her own catering firm.

Carolyn has had feature and travel articles published, writes romantic suspense novels, and works as a paralegal. She has a son and two daughters and cooks for a food-loving husband who must watch his weight and cholesterol.

Pepper Durcholz

In 1987 Pepper Durcholz went to the doctor with a bladder infection and returned home a diabetic. Diabetes called for a drastic change in her eating habits, and she does love to eat. She teamed up with her neighbor, Alberta Gentry, who had been a diabetic for several years, and Carolyn Williamson to compile recipes that were tasty and appropriate for diabetics and heart patients.

With four kids and a husband to cook for, Pepper has lots of tasters to try her new dishes. She has been a professional temporary for nine years, and she also sings, knits, crochets, sews, does ceramics, decorates cakes, makes fancy candies, and writes historical romance and romantic suspense.

Alberta Gentry

The only symptom or warning she had was in 1981, when her vision became fuzzy for no apparent reason. After a test for diabetes, she went into the hospital for tests and to monitor her blood count. Two weeks later she left with better knowledge of three things every diabetic should know to stay alive and healthy: exercise, medication, and the proper food.

Since becoming a diabetic with a growing family to cook for, Alberta has developed new recipes that she can eat and serve to her family. She is writing a historical romance and a regency romance novel.